6/25

" I never found a kindlier people"
The Early History
of
Christian Science
in
Vermont

Vermont Schoolhouse Press
Chester, Vermont

Copyright 1996 by
Cynthia Parsons

Vermont Schoolhouse Press
PO Box 516. Chester, VT 05143

All rights reserved
Printed in the United State of America

Accura Printing
South Barre, VT

Library of Congress Catalog Card Number: 96-61405

ISBN 0-9617872-8-7

Historian: Leona Griffin, Winooski, VT
Illustrations: Craig Rankin, Cavendish, VT
Typesetting: Kathleen Whalen, Chester, VT

AVAILABLE

Misty Valley Books
On the Green
P.O. Box 700
Chester, VT 05143

802-875-3400
FAX 802-875-3411

Contents

Preface i

Section One
    First the Seeds 1

Section Two
    Vermont at the Turn-of-the-Century . 37

Section Three
    Branch by Branch 61

Section Four
    Fruitage 137

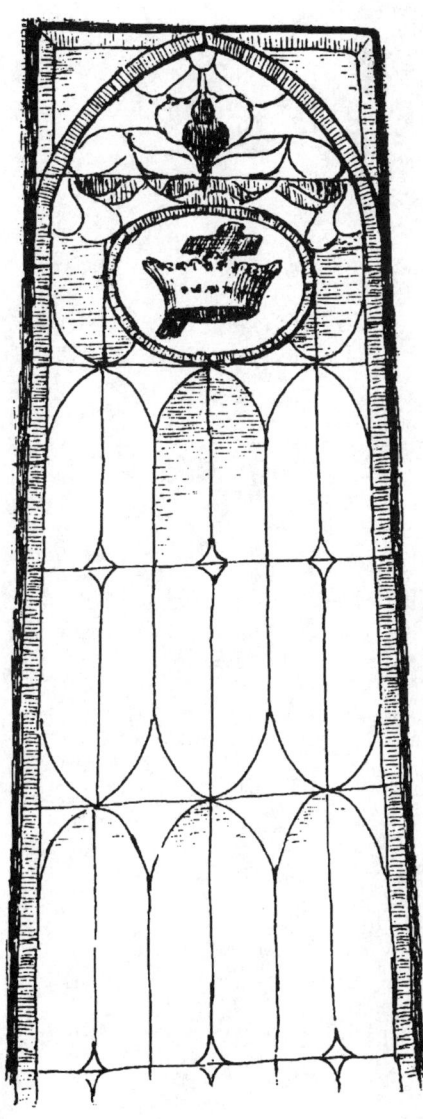

Preface

This brief history is the work of many. The children, grandchildren, and great grandchildren of some of the early Christian Scientists have scoured old files for information. Anecdotes have come forth from multiple sources. Church members have gone through bound volumes of the Sentinel and Journal page by page looking for "Vermont" datelines. Present clerks, and former clerks have dug into old files, opened up closed vaults, visited attic corners, and searched memories to enlighten and enliven this work.

The Mother Church History Department has patiently answered query after query.

In 1888, Mrs. Eddy gave an address in Chicago to The National Christian Scientists' Association (1886-1892) whose purpose was, as the March 1886 issue of *The Christian Science Journal* stated, "...to bring together and place upon an equal footing with one another in Christian Science, all students thereof...and so to promote unity and brotherly love."

The Church of Christ (Scientist) was established in Boston in 1879 and reorganized in 1892 as The First Church of Christ, Scientist.

Mrs. Eddy concluded her 1888 address with the following expectation: "Christian Science and Christian Scientists will, *must*, have a history; and if I could write the history in poor parody of Tennyson's grand verse, it would read thus":

> Traitors to right of them,
> M.D.'s to left of them,
> Priestcraft in front of them,
>   volleyed and thundered!
> Into the jaws of hate,
> Out through the door of Love,
> On to the blest above,
>   Marched the one hundred.

And in <u>Science and Health with Key to the Scriptures</u> Mrs. Eddy declares, "The history of our country, like all history, illustrates the might of Mind...."

This little story of the early history of Christian Science in Vermont does illustrate the might of ideas, the planting of seeds, the cultivating of the branches, and the fruitage therefrom.

Today, one hundred ten years after the first Scientists gathered together to found a church in St. Johnsbury, <u>The Christian Science Journal</u> lists three nurses, five practitioners, and thirteen branches throughout Vermont. Our history includes hundreds -- no thousands -- of authenticated testimonials to the healing power of Christian Science.

We got up early; our branches are budding.

SECTION ONE
FIRST THE SEEDS

In Barton, Vermont

In Montpelier and Waterbury, Vermont

In Barre, Vermont

Throughout Vermont

Vermont's Students

Vermont's Testifiers

Vermont's Committees on Publication

Vermont's Teachers and Practitioners

Vermont's Lecturers

 Christian Science

Vermont's Newspapers

Vermont's Churches and Societies

Vermonters at Pleasant View and Chestnut Hill

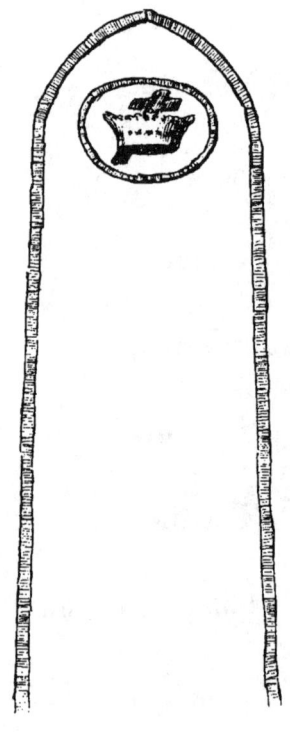

First the Seeds

The seeds of Truth fall by the wayside, on artless listeners. They fall on stony ground and shallow soil. The fowls of the air pick them up. Much of what has been sown has withered away, but what remaineth has fallen into the good and honest hearts and is bearing fruit.

Mary Baker Eddy

In Barton, Vermont...

The first lecture ever given on Christian Science in Vermont was delivered in the Methodist Church in Barton, in Vermont's Northeast Kingdom, on July 24, 1882, at 7.30 in the evening by the founder of The Mother Church, The First Church of Christ, Scientist, Mary Baker Eddy.

At the invitation of one of her early workers, Arthur T. Buswell, Mrs. Eddy and a teen-age Sunday School pupil came to spend from July 10 to August 3, 1882, in Barton, Vermont, in his family home. Barton is less than twenty miles south of the Canadian border, and some thirty-five miles north of St. Johnsbury.

This was a very key time in the beginnings of Christian Science worldwide. A Vermonter from Londonderry, Asa Gilbert Eddy, Mrs. Eddy's devoted co-worker and husband since January 1, 1877, had passed away on June 3, 1882, during one of the most tumultuous times in Mrs. Eddy's life.

Apparently it took three days for Mrs. Eddy and her companion to get from Back Bay Boston to Barton, Vermont. We do not know her exact route, but we do know she came by train; and we know that she spent the first night in Concord, then, most probably, came across New Hampshire to either St. Johnsbury (using the Twin State Rail Road) or to White River Junction (on the Boston and Maine line). Then the final leg of the journey on the Canadian Pacific RR line. And presumably she had to spend another three days returning to Boston where Clara Choate and Julia Bartlett were "holding the fort." During the time Mrs. Eddy was in Barton she took a round-trip train ride with her young companion to Newport, on the shore of Lake Memphremagog. On her way back to Boston, she spent the night of August 3, in St. Johnsbury.

Arthur Buswell apparently handled all the travel arrangements, including transfers by coach for the passengers and the luggage between accommodations and trains. The original invoice indicates that he not only charged Mrs. Eddy for the actual costs, but took

an additional fee for himself for handling the arrangements.

During this summer vacation, she developed plans to publish a religious periodical, what we know today as The Christian Science Journal. The minutes of the Christian Scientists' Association show that on January 31, 1883, they established the Christian Scientists' Publishing Company "for the purpose of preparing a publication for the good of the Cause." The first volume appeared in April 1883, and it became a monthly in August 1884. Practitioners and teachers could submit a "card" advertising their healing services. Mrs. Eddy and thirteen others advertised in the first edition. A Mrs. Mary F. Berry in Manchester, New Hampshire, was the only practitioner listed outside Massachusetts; her announcement included the information: "Absent treatment a specialty."

The February 1885 edition of the Journal carried an advertisement for the first Vermonter, Ellen E. Cross who lived near St. Johnsbury. The second Vermonter, Mrs. T.H. Hale was listed for just ten months between July 1885 and April 1886. The third, Mrs. Mary E. Morse, had her first listing in Brattleboro in November 1885. In all, between 1885 and 1900, Vermont had twenty-three practitioners, and by 1907, three teachers. [See Section 4]

In early 1884, a pupil of Mrs. Eddy's, Julia Bartlett, visited Littleton, New Hampshire, where she did healing work and taught a Primary Class. We know Miss Bartlett taught a class in Vermont in March 1884, and believe she came at least one other time between 1886 and 1889, but do not know either the dates or the locations where she taught. We do know that she stayed in Alethea Warren's home [See Section 4, May

1894, for listing of Mrs. Mary Waite Warren]. But do not know whether that was while Alethea Warren lived in West Georgia, ten miles south of St. Albans, or in St. Albans, itself. Several of the earliest practitioners in Vermont took class instruction from Miss Bartlett. Of this worker who started her study of Christian Science in 1880, and served in Mrs. Eddy's household and then The Mother Church as an original member of the Bible Lesson Committee for more than twenty-five years starting in 1889, the historian Clifford P. Smith declared that "she was a woman of unswerving faithfulness and consecration."

While in Barton, Mrs. Eddy, according to one historian, often sat on the back porch, observing a large oak tree which became the inspiration for one of the poems she chose to place in her book of poems. It is titled, "The Oak on the Mountain's Summit." [See "Poems" chapter in Prose Works.] This was not Mrs. Eddy's first trip to Vermont. When she was twenty-two years old, she took a trip from Bow, New Hampshire, to Littleton, and then across the Connecticut River to the town of Newbury in Vermont. She wrote about the trip in the journal she kept since early childhood.

The Mother Church History Department has allowed me to quote from a few of the letters Mrs. Eddy wrote while in Barton. The code in brackets following each quotation identifies the archival source. The following excerpt from a letter she wrote on July 16th during her visit to Barton to one of her pupils, Mrs. Clara E. Choate, hints at the struggle which brought her to Vermont the summer of 1882:

> I am up among the towering heights of this verdant state, green with the leaves of earth and fresh with the fragrance of good will and human

kindness. I never found a kindlier people. I am situated as pleasantly as I can be in the absence of the <u>one true heart</u> that has been so much to me. O, darling I never shall master this point of missing him all the time I do believe, but I can try, and am trying as I must -- to sever all the chords that bind me to person or things material. [L04089]

On July 19, she wrote to Julia Bartlett:

It is beautiful here the hills, vales and lakes are lovely. But this was his native state and <u>he is not here.</u> [L07691]

On July 27 she wrote to a Mrs. Clarke, one of her pupils, sharing with her some of her sadness over the passing of Gilbert, as she referred to Mr. Eddy.

I confess to feeling weary of earth's woes and heaven laden; but I also find a holy shrine and inviolate, where I can bring my wounded heart, and bathe my wings in Love.... Trust, dear one, if you cannot see, and your faith will save you, and when your faith is tried and proved He will bless you with all needed good and deliver you from error. [Signed] "Lovingly, M B G Eddy." [L04664]

Also on July 27 she wrote to Mrs. Choate, obviously much improved since her letter to her of the 16th:

Hold the Fort, for I am coming.... Be wise as a serpent and harmless as the doves that are cooing over my window. I hope my forty days in the wilderness are about over....My lecture made a big stir. A Rev. Methodist called on me the next day and talked pretty much all the A. M., and an M.D. talks of studying. [L04090]

On July 28, she wrote to another pupil, a James Ackland:

> I love this mountain scenery and see in its rock-rib[b]ed rest a home for the raven's callow brood, but not for me. The world was for others [.] It was not for me [.] I was made a lone isle in life's desolate sea. [L10643]

The Mother Church History Department noted in a letter to me May 9, 1995: "Church History is not aware of any student taking up healing work in Barton as a result of Mrs. Eddy's time there." Yet by 1886, there were enough Christian Scientists in the St. Johnsbury area to begin the formation of a Society which became a branch in 1898. And in Montpelier, a Society was formed in 1888, which became a branch in 1905. In the small town of Calais, north of Montpelier and Barre in 1882, the Ainsworth family were identified as Christian Scientists; as were their friends the Standishes who lived in the Montpelier area.

In Montpelier, and Waterbury, Vermont...

William Clark and Ebenezer Foster (both of whom later took class instruction from Mrs. Eddy) served together in the Civil War. Foster was a drummer boy, just sixteen years old in 1863. Foster was one of eleven children born and brought up in Moretown, Vermont, a sheep-raising area close to Waterbury and Montpelier. His father was a devout

member of the Methodist Episcopal Church, as were most of his eleven children, including Ebenezer.

After the Civil War, Ebenezer studied homeopathic medicine in Philadelphia, and by 1870 was a homeopathic physician with an office in Waterbury Center. We don't know the exact date, but probably early in 1887, when Foster learned that his friend Will Clark was seriously ill, he went to Montpelier to call on him, and was surprised when he came to the door himself obviously well. His friend had been healed by reading <u>Science and Health</u>.

Foster was able to borrow a copy of the textbook from a fellow Methodist, and before the end of the year he had gone to Boston in order to meet Mrs. Eddy who invited him to take Primary class instruction with her in 1887. And in 1888, both Foster and Clark, as well as Mrs. Mary Shipman Dillingham, the woman who loaned him his first copy of the textbook, took Normal class instruction from Mrs. Eddy; Foster also went through an 1889 Normal class. Mrs. Eddy was much impressed by this Vermont physician who quickly adopted Christian Science arguing that it was the higher mind-cure for which homeopathic *materia medica* was his stepping-stone.

In May, 1888, he delivered a paper at the annual meeting of the Vermont State Homeopathic Medical Society, excerpts of which appeared in Volume II, No. 2, of the <u>Christian Science Series</u> -- a magazine published by the Christian Scientists' Association from 1889 to 1891. In that paper he referred to Mrs. M.B.G. Eddy as a "homeopathic practitioner." Quoting her that "Divine Mind and its ideas are the only realities," he went on to declare:

From Homeopathy has sprung another evolution which, in its power to reform, to heal, and to renew, is far greater; while its scope is far wider. It steps entirely out of and beyond the material and sensual into the wholly mental and spiritual. Its stately strides will be felt not only in the medical field, but in the theological world also. It is a harbinger of universal peace and harmony....

I took a course of instruction at Massachusetts Metaphysical College, presided over by Rev. Mrs. Eddy. Since coming from the Metaphysical College I have administered only mental medicine and with much better results than I ever obtained from material medicine in like cases.

Mrs. Eddy invited him to join her in Boston, and in November, 1888, having gained permission from his father, Leonard Robertson Foster, she gave this forty-one year old physician the name "Eddy." For the next decade he used the name "E. J. Foster Eddy," and placed the following initials after his name: "M.D., C.S.D." As far as we have been able to determine, Foster Eddy was never listed in the Journal as a practitioner, though he did teach three classes in the Metaphysical College. From 1893 to 1896 he was Mrs. Eddy's designated publisher. At this time, Mrs. Eddy's several books were in great demand, and she was still revising the textbook.

Mrs. Eddy, in 1888, was still hopeful that the mainline Christian churches would adopt the teachings of Christian Science on sickness as well as sin, and that the medical profession would embrace Christian Science healing. The Christian Science churches in Boston and elsewhere, still had preachers, not readers. When the fiftieth edition of the textbook was published in 1891, Reverend Lanson P. Norcross was still the

Vermont

pastor of the Christian Science congregation in Boston which met in Chickering Hall. It wasn't until 1895 that Mrs. Eddy designated the Bible and <u>Science & Health With Key to the Scriptures</u> as the Pastor for both The Mother Church and all the branches.

In 1888, when Mrs. Eddy spent most of August in the White Mountains at a resort in Fabyan, New Hampshire, Foster Eddy and Calvin Frye went with her, and both served as her secretary to help her meet the demands of an enormous amount of correspondence. By the following summer, Mrs. Eddy was looking for a place to live outside Boston -- away from the demands of the church's headquarters. She wished to retire from her work at the Metaphysical College and as the Pastor of the Church of Christ, Scientist, in Boston.

In Barre, Vermont...

Once again she turned to Vermont; this time it was Foster Eddy who chose the location. He rented a house in the center of Barre on the edge of the public park, and when the schools let out and the band tuned up for the summer, Mrs. Eddy left Barre and after considering several other sites finally settled in Concord, New Hampshire.

The story is told of a neighbor in Barre who warned his daughter that Mrs. Eddy was a wicked woman because of her strange religious beliefs. This

little twelve-year old was curious as to what the lady might be like, so she garnered two of her young friends and when her father was not at home walked down the street to where Mrs. Eddy was visiting. Mrs. Eddy, so the report states, was reading on the porch, but when the girls approached she got up and began chatting with them. In a few minutes, she was picking some of the flowers growing in a border, and presented each of the little girls with a bouquet of summer beauty. Who told this story? The little girl, Eva Rogers, who, as an adult -- Mrs. Eva Rogers Travers -- wrote about the incident to The Mother Church.

Foster Eddy had a rocky time in the church. For some eight years, he lived in Boston and worked for the central church organization, a few times joining Mrs. Eddy's household, and served as one of her corresponding secretaries taking messages back and forth from Concord to Boston. He helped with the publishing effort, and took cases as a practitioner. Dr. Eddy (as he preferred to be addressed) had five articles published in the Journal: two in Volume 8 (pp. 47 & 141), one in Volume 9 (pg. 235), one in Volume 11 (pg. 348), and his final one in Volume 13 (pg. 441).

After he had taught two classes in the Metaphysical College (besides Mrs. Eddy, only Asa G. Eddy, General Erastus N. Bates, and Foster Eddy taught at the college), Mrs. Eddy expressed concern about the correctness of his teaching. Nevertheless, he taught a third class, and after interviewing several of the pupils who had been in the class, including James Gilman the artist, she did not permit Foster Eddy to teach again.

He moved in 1896 to the Philadelphia area and for a time was busy with branch church activities, but was fairly soon voted out of the branch he had joined.

He traveled in the western territories, visited the Grand Canyon, probably visited family members in Wisconsin, but before the turn of the century he was back in Vermont apparently practicing homeopathic medicine in Waterbury Center. On March 6, 1907, he received a gift of $45,000 from Mrs. Eddy for agreeing not to contest her will which would leave the bulk of her estate to The First Church of Christ, Scientist, except for a few special bequests. Instead of honoring that agreement, he was one of the signers of a legal brief called "The Next Friends Suit," which attempted to wrest all Mrs. Eddy's property from her. That suit eventually was withdrawn. And even though he had signed a paper in 1907 agreeing not to contest her will, when it was probated early in 1911 -- and in which he received another $5,000 -- he did anyway. That effort also was defeated.

Because Foster Eddy was a Vermont native, many of the state's newspapers covered the activities of The Mother Church, particularly noting the several public trials directed against Mrs. Eddy. Reviewing several archival containers affectionately dubbed "shoe boxes" full of old newspaper clippings from the turn of the century, more reports were favorable to Mrs. Eddy and to the early efforts to establish branch churches throughout Vermont than were critical. When Mrs. Eddy passed away, most of the Vermont papers carried editorials praising her courage and leadership abilities.

A few, again because of Foster Eddy's relationship as Mrs. Eddy's adopted son, played up the financial picture, interviewing Foster about his earlier gift of $45,000, and final gift of $5,000.

Arthur Buswell, whose family home it was that Mrs. Eddy visited in 1882, and who was expelled from

the Christian Scientists' Association in 1886, did not return to Vermont.

Throughout Vermont...

While Buswell's and Foster's rocky soil did not remain "kindlier" for Mrs. Eddy or the Church she founded, Christian Science was finding good soil in farm houses and village homes throughout Vermont. In the *Journal* for July 1890, under the heading, "Reports from the Field," was this enthusiastic endorsement:

> I have a copy of Science and Health and would not exchange it for all minor literature, could I not get another, much as I enjoy reading what I have been able to secure. Science and Health is a whole library in itself, and always new. It cannot fail to enlighten, elevate, and alleviate all who earnestly peruse its pages. -- Mrs. E.W., Morrisville, Vt.

By 1898, just sixteen years after Mrs. Eddy's lecture in Barton, Vermont had eighteen practitioners listed in the *Journal*. In fact, Vermont had more practitioners than some twenty-one other states, including Alabama, Florida, Maryland, Virginia, and Rhode Island. These healers lived in Barre, Brattleboro, Burlington, Essex Junction, Montpelier, McIndoe Falls, Rochester, Rutland, St. Albans, St. Johnsbury, and West Randolph. [See Section 4] A contemporary Vermont writer, Howard Frank Mosher, has described the "good soil" of Vermont's northern reaches as "still characterized by a rough-and-tumble egalitarianism

and the kind of appreciation for individualism and variety that our democracy grew out of." It is not too much of a stretch to state that the same "individualism and variety" nurtured the early seeds, out of which grew Vermont's Christian Science movement.

A young school teacher and primitive artist, James Franklin Gilman, who spent summers traveling throughout Vermont bartering room and board for drawings of family farms and homesteads, became interested in Christian Science in 1884. In 1891, he began doing healing work, and that year he had two articles printed in the Journal [Volume 9, pages 326 and 380]. In 1892 he left his teaching position, travelled to Concord, New Hampshire, in mid December and was hired by a photographer working for Mrs. Eddy to make sketches of her home known as Pleasant View. On New Years Day, 1893, he and the photographer were invited to have dinner with Mrs. Eddy. She found him a ready and willing student of Christian Science. He took Primary class instruction for a week in mid-January, and in March, Mrs. Eddy engaged him to illustrate a poem she had written during January and February.

Gilman was in the class Foster Eddy taught in 1893, and he was one of the pupils she interviewed afterwards to discover that her adopted son was not teaching correctly.

Gilman worked on the drawings for *Christ and Christmas* for some six months, and the little book was finally published in December 1893 in time for Christmas sales. It received praise from some and vigorous condemnation from others. The drawings -- more than the text -- were so controversial that Mrs. Eddy withdrew the book from publication on January

19, 1894. Then, with some alterations of the illustrations, she reissued it in December 1897.

When he left Concord, Gilman moved first to Gardner, Massachusetts, and then nearby to Athol, and in 1899 was a listed practitioner in Athol. He continued writing for the periodicals, and was published in the Journals of 1891, 1893, and 1896; a Sentinel article appeared in 1900. [For further information about Gilman the artist, see James Franklin Gilman: Nineteenth Century Painter, by Adele Godchaux Dawson (Canaan, NH: Phoenix Publishers, 1975).]

Meanwhile, the branches were beginning to form. In 1898, Sunday services were held in Essex Junction and Randolph. And in Barre, Burlington, and St. Johnsbury, the churches held Wednesday meetings as well as Sunday services. Barre and St. Johnsbury had Sunday schools and Burlington a public Reading Room.

It was in 1898, that Mrs. Eddy ruled that branches should hold their "experience" meetings on Wednesdays instead of Fridays. To quote the official announcement: "Hereafter the Wednesday experience meeting will be made throughout the Field a meeting of interests on subjects pertaining to Christian Science, as well as personal experience, and will be called the *Wednesday Evening Meeting*."

Two years after Mrs. Eddy visited Barton and gave a lecture on Christian Science there, Nell Shipman of Montpelier learned of the healing of her husband's sister (Emily Shipman Wells of Lisbon, New Hampshire), went to Boston in 1888 to study with Mrs. Eddy, and was healed of a long-standing shoulder problem. Nell Shipman was one of the founders of the

Montpelier Society. She was an active practitioner in the area for a quarter of a century.

Her husband's niece (Emma Shipman) lived in Danville, Vermont, and when her Aunt Nell was visiting her home her father's hand was seriously injured. Rather than have a finger amputated, he agreed to Christian Science treatment from his sister-in-law and his finger was restored. Emma began reading the textbook -- a gift from her Aunt Nell -- and was healed of asthma and sick headaches. [See Section 4]

While Emma went to college in Boston, and taught in The Mother Church Sunday School for some fifty years, she was a frequent visitor to Vermont; many members of her family were active in Vermont's Societies and Branches. Her first metaphysical article appeared in the Sentinel in 1899; the first in the Journal in 1900. Between 1899 and 1958, she had more than thirty articles published in the church magazines.

Emma Shipman was taught by Mrs. Eddy, and served The Mother Church for one year (1949-1950) as president. Her grandfather -- Nell Shipman's father-in-law -- was a Congregational (or Methodist) minister in Montpelier in the mid eighteen hundreds; five of his six children became Christian Scientists before the turn of the century, helping to establish churches in Vermont, New Hampshire, and Massachusetts.

Emma Shipman's Aunt, Mary Shipman Dillingham, when Mrs. Eddy was living at Pleasant View, sent her some maple sugar from the Dillingham Farm. Mrs. Eddy sent back her thanks, "...for sweet things of the earth and heaven."

Vermont's Students...

The early seeds of Christian Science continued to take root in Vermont. In 1888, four Vermonters went to the Massachusetts Metaphysical College in Boston to study with Mrs. Eddy, paying $300 for three weeks of instruction. They were:

- Ebenezer J. Foster, M.D.
- Mrs. Nell Shipman, who returned to teach in Vermont.
- William Clark, who returned to Vermont but did not receive permission from Mrs. Eddy to teach, but served her briefly as a gardener at Pleasant View.
- Mrs. Mary Dillingham, no record of her practicing in Vermont.

In the August 1897 issue of the Journal is a report from First Church, Barre, about the placing of Science and Health in the following local libraries:

Barre - French Library
Burlington - Fletcher and University Libraries
Bennington - Soldier's Home Library
Calais - Free Library
Georgia - Free Library
Montpelier - Kellogg-Hubbard Library
Pittsford - Free Library
Poultney - Town Library
Randolph Centre - State Normal School
West Randolph - Public and Ladies' Library

Rochester - Public Library
Rutland - Y.M.C.A. and Public Libraries
West Rutland - Public Library
St. Albans - Public Library
St. Johnsbury - Y.M.C.A. and Public Libraries

Vermont's Testifiers...

The first testimony published in the Journal which we might stretch a point to be by a "Vermonter," appeared in 1894. It was written by a Mrs. Isabel Shackelford, who was in the practice in Brattleboro for two years (1900-1902), but it refers to a healing accomplished while she was living in Pennsylvania. After her time in Brattleboro, she returned to Pennsylvania. Her brief testimony stated:

> A coal miner who had been quite deaf for 18 years came to me for treatment one Sunday morning. He staid [sic] to the Bible class and heard the lesson well. Upon going home he heard a clock tick in the room adjoining the one he was sitting in. In a short time he could hear as well as anyone.
>
> A very serious claim which he did not tell me of was healed during treatment for other troubles and reported to me afterwards. He has interested many whom he knows by reporting his healing and they have come for treatment. I hope to open a reading room soon.

If she was not the first Vermonter to testify, then Elmer Goding, C.S., a member of the Randolph Church

qualifies. His testimony was published in the August 1897 Journal dealing with what apparently was a criticism about the high cost of the text-book. He quoted the testimony given at one of the Randolph Society's Wednesday meetings by "a lady" -- no other identification was given. Her report:

> After being treated by several physicians, and trying all kinds of patent medicine, gradually growing worse, my husband heard of Christian Science, and bought a copy of Science and Health, and brought it home, saying, "I want you to read this book, it may heal you."
>
> I said, "How much did you pay for it?"
>
> "Three dollars and eight cents," was his reply.
>
> "A fool and his money are soon parted," I answered. "What do you think the book could do for me?"
>
> "Read it and see."
>
> I laid it aside, thinking it was wrong to throw away so much money when we so needed it. The more I thought of it, the more I thought I must read it, as he had paid so much for it. If it had been only fifty cents or a dollar I would have left it unread.
>
> I commenced reading it, and had not finished before I was healed, physically and morally, and am to-day a well woman, doing my own work and instead of my home being of wretchedness it is one of peace and joy. And the "little book" has wrought this transformation. I want to say that if I could not get another copy, a thousand dollars would not purchase this one.

> If at any time I seem a little tired, my little girls will say, "Mamma, you had better read your book."

Thus Mr. Goding concludes the testimony: "This is only one of the many instances that I might name showing that our text-book is above price."

In 1905, eight years after the above purchase was made for $3.08, the cost of the least expensive copy of Science and Health was $3.18. The Concordance to the textbook was $5.00, Miscellaneous Writings was $2.25, and the Manual was $1.00. The Journal was $.20/copy; the Sentinel $.03/copy. The cloth edition of the Christian Science Hymnal was $1.15. The shorter books, such at Unity of Good, Rudimental Divine Science, the Messages for 1900, 1901, and 1902 were all less than $1.00.

The next testimony published in the Journal carrying a Vermont dateline -- that is, the next one we have located -- appears in March, 1899, and was written by C.C. Sabin of Richford, a town some sixteen miles west of Newport. He states:

> I have been a traveling salesman for forty years. I was healed through Christian Science of inherited semi-monthly headaches, bronchial difficulty of a distressing nature, and last, but not least, of hernia. I have overcome seeming death in relapse from pneumonia, a broken shoulder, cancer, and many other claims.

Vermont's Committees on Publication...

In 1900, Mrs. Eddy established an international program to support and defend -- "in a Christian manner" -- public statements about Christian Science. Each state and each nation would have an individual chosen by the Christian Scientists in each area and approved by the Directors of The Mother Church who would monitor public statements, provide corrections where necessary, and work to support the rights of Church members in federal and state governing bodies to preserve the right of Christian Scientists to use prayer as a healing agent. These were known as "Committees on Publication," or C.O.P. We believe that the first person appointed to be the C.O.P. in Vermont was George P. Moore of St. Johnsbury in 1903. Most probably, he was the husband of Mrs. Harriet J. Moore, a listed practitioner.

If we are correct, he was followed by Helen Ross of Rutland, Frank E. Bowman of Essex Junction, Frank Walker, a practitioner in Barre, Charles E. Peck of St. Johnsbury, Arthur C. Whitney of Burlington, Hulda J. Hoag also of Burlington, Ellis W. Moore of St. Johnsbury, Rachel A. Banister (no known location), and then by Mrs. Eunice Dizer, a practitioner in Bellows Falls. Next to serve was Mildred Drew of Montpelier who had served in the Vermont Legislature for several terms. She was followed by Virgil Collins of St. Johnsbury. They did their work well. The Mother Church legal department (today known as the Office of the General Counsel) has agreed that they know of no instance of any legal action against Christian Scientists or the practice of Christian Science throughout Vermont during these early years.

Vermont

A ruling on October 6, 1903, by the Supreme Court of New Hampshire found for the defendant, Irving C. Tomlinson, -- then First Reader in the Concord Christian Science Church. For three years, Mr. Tomlinson was charged with negligence for treating a case of appendicitis with prayer instead of medicine. The Supreme Court concluded: "We cannot say as a matter of law that Christian Science is a humbug." Reportedly, this ruling influenced the healing work in Vermont which went unchallenged in its courts.

In June, 1904, while Mrs. Eddy was living at Pleasant View, she invited Christian Scientists who were attending the Sunday service in the Original Mother Church to come the afternoon of June 13, to see the Concord Church edifice. We know that Emma Shipman of Danville was there that afternoon with 2,000 other Christian Scientists. [See My: 171-172.]

In 1906, a bill was introduced in the Vermont Legislature to, as the November 16 issue of the Montpelier Evening Argus stated, "permit Christian Scientists to treat diseases in Vermont." The Barre Times put it this way, "Whether or not Christian Scientists should be allowed to practice their religious healing in Vermont was considered by the general committee of the House last night." And the Burlington Free Press, the same day wrote: "Christian Science was on trial tonight before the House general committee when the bill introduced by Mr. Bailey of Essex was under consideration."

Among those speaking for the bill was the superintendent of the Montpelier water department. To quote from the Evening Argus:

F.S. Smith...told the committee he was cured of consumption by Christian Science. Thirteen years ago he had hemorrhages and doctors gave him up. As a last resort, he visited a Christian Science healer. Within the past year he has taken out insurance and his lungs had been pronounced sound by six physicians.

Apparently the Christian Scientists prevailed.

It was in 1902 that Mrs. Eddy established a special Church service for Thanksgiving. The Journal for November 1902, gives the order of service including the use of the annual Thanksgiving Day Proclamation issued by the President of the United States. That first year, the subject of the special lesson sermon was "Giving Thanks," and consisted of five sections, shortening the reading time so that: "Testimonies by members of the church, appropriate for the occasion" might be given. A note accompanied the special Thanksgiving Day citations stating that: "...For the convenience of students using editions of Science and Health prior to the 226th, the following references are added, giving the pages corresponding to those in the revised edition..."

We have found no record of when any of the Vermont branches began holding their Thanksgiving services, but Barre, Burlington, Randolph, Rutland, and St. Johnsbury all might have done so in 1902, as they had already become "recognized" by The Mother Church.

Vermont's Teachers and Practitioners...

By 1902, there were nineteen practitioners in eleven towns. In 1905, Vermont had sixteen practitioners in Barnard, Barre, Brattleboro, Burlington, North Clarendon, Montpelier, Randolph, Rutland, St. Albans, St. Johnsbury, and West Georgia. For a bit of perspective, we looked to see where and how many practitioners were listed outside North America.

England	57
Germany	14
Scotland	12
France	8
Ireland	4
Switzerland	4
China	3
Denmark	1
Holland	1
India	1
Norway	1
Philippines	1

By 1907, there were three teachers of Christian Science located in Barre, Montpelier, and Rutland; and some seventeen Journal-listed practitioners in Barnard, Barre, Burlington, Essex Junction, Montpelier, Randolph, Rutland, St. Albans, and St. Johnsbury. [See Section 4]

By 1910, there were fourteen Societies and Branch Churches in Bennington, Brattleboro, Bellows Falls,

Springfield, and Wilmington in the southern part of the state; in Montpelier, Randolph, Barre, and Rutland in the middle; and in St. Johnsbury, Burlington, Newport, St. Albans, and Lyndonville in the north.

Vermont's Lecturers...

The second public lecture on Christian Science (counting Mrs. Eddy's talk in July 1882 as the first) was held, if our records are correct, on November 24, 1898, by William McKenzie in St. Johnsbury. Mr. McKenzie lectured in Burlington the following year on October 24, and the fourth lecture was given in Barre on August 17, 1900, by the Honorable William G. Ewing. Judge Ewing was introduced by the Vermont Secretary of State, the Honorable F. A. Howland. We have a record from the October 24, 1900 issue of the Sentinel that Rev. Wm. P. McKenzie gave a lecture in Barre. This makes the lecture given in the Music Hall in St. Johnsbury on January 31, 1901, by Irving C. Tomlinson, then a member of the Board of Directors, the fifth. A local practitioner and the first Committee on Publication, George P. Moore gave the introduction. The Randolph Society gave its first lecture on October 31, 1902.

A year later, September 13, 1903, again in the Music Hall in St. Johnsbury, the lecturer was Carol Norton from New York City, a pupil of Mrs. Eddy's, whose topic was: "Christian Science, The Gospel of Righteousness and of Health." He was introduced by a local minister who exhibited broad-mindedness,

perhaps with a little tongue-in-cheek. The Reverend A.F. Walch said, in part:

> However we may differ in our individual opinions upon the great matters of faith and life, we are yet all hoping from the bottom of our hearts that our Christian Science friends may be right in their claim that they have discovered the way that shall lead to bodily as well as spiritual well-being.... It is always well to be able to see the good in others, and to recognize that it is a God-given right to follow the dictates of reason and consciousness.

A year later, October 10, 1904, the St. Johnsbury branch gave another public lecture; the speaker was Bicknell Young. The introduction began thusly:

> Ladies, Gentlemen, Brethren of the Christian Science Church: For the second time it becomes my pleasant duty to stand on this platform (Rev. Walch in the Music Hall) and welcome to the generous hearing of a St. Johnsbury audience a speaker of the faith of Christian Science. I do this gladly because I believe good will come from the full and free discussion of the subject at hand...
>
> I believe our Christian Science brethren are trying to live up to their doctrine and that they are succeeding is sufficiently proven by the fact that their faith works the most wonderful transformation in their lives.

Vermont's Newspapers...

The Rutland Herald, on December 23, 1908, carried a fairly long editorial discussing Christian Science. They posed the following hypothetical question using "two men" in a discussion. One asks, "Are you a Christian Scientist?" To which the other replies, "No, I am a scientific Christian." The editorial plays that idea back and forth, but concludes on a positive note quoting Elbert Hubbard: "Even the most bigoted and prejudiced now agree that the cures of Christian Scientists are genuine." The very next day the Rutland Herald praised Christian Science under the headline, "Groping For Truth." On April 4, 1907, again the Rutland Herald carried an editorial of prescient concern. To quote a portion:

> We have a good deal of tolerance for Christian Scientists. If their faith helps them, spiritually and physically, why, let it. We are satisfied that it does.
>
> That it is mostly a hoax, in its assumption of divine authorization we also believe. Mrs. Eddy was a shrewd and practical woman who developed a physical truth or two and clothed it with the mantle of prophetess. The thing has been done before and will be again.

That claim of "hoax" was addressed by Mrs. Eddy in her book, *The First Church of Christ Scientist and Miscellany* on pages 359-60. Unfortunately one of Mrs. Eddy's pupils, Augusta Stetson, was claiming divinity for Mrs. Eddy as well as herself. In that regard, The Barre Times ran a two-sentence editorial on December 28, 1910, just after Mrs. Eddy passing, which one can only wonder whether it was written by one of those

stalwart early students of Christian Science living in the Barre area. We quote it in full.

> Mrs. Augusta Stetson is scoring up for Mrs. Eddy's place by announcing that she has the power of divination which is denied the men who are now in charge of the Christian Science Church. Would it be too irreverent to remark that she is talking through her Stetson?

When the "Next Friends" suit was withdrawn, proof that Mrs. Eddy was not only alive but in command of her business interests and mentally alert was carried in all of Vermont's daily papers and many of its weeklies. For example, strong and complimentary articles appeared in the Barre Times, Barton Monitor, the Bellows Falls Times, the Bennington Banner, the Bradford Opinion, the Brandon Union, the Brattleboro Phoenix, the Burlington Free Press, the Montpelier Watchman, Randolph Herald, Rutland News, St. Albans Messenger, St. Johnsbury Caledonian, and the Windsor Journal. Weekly papers served by the Essex Publishing Company also carried reports in Charlotte, Essex Junction, Grand Isle, Jericho, Milton, Richmond, and Winooski.

Vermont's Churches and Societies...

In Section Two - Branch by Branch, we discover that St. Johnsbury bought their church building as early as 1918, twenty-four years after the Original Mother Church building was completed in 1894, and twelve

years after the Extension was built. Yet, as early as 1910, Barre, Brattleboro, Randolph, Rutland, and St. Johnsbury each had at least one practitioner, a Reading Room, Sunday School, Sunday services, Wednesday Testimony Meetings, and sufficient members to be known as a First Church of Christ, Scientist. Bennington, Essex Junction (Burlington), Lyndonville, Montpelier, and St. Albans were Societies. The following were First Readers at that time: Mrs. Rose F. Walker, Mrs. Fanny G. Miles, Primus P. Lamson, Miss Fannie C. Wilcox, Miss Kate D. Peck, Mrs. Harriet Hovey Rogers, Mrs. Clara E. Drury, Miss Cora W. Frasier, Charles H. Shipman, and Mrs. Anna B. Hale. A year later, a Society was formed in Barnard with Miss Earlie Sacred Chase as First Reader, and another in Wilmington, William N. Bassett the First Reader.

If we are correct, Vermont has had twenty branch churches/societies. Thirteen are still active today. Those which have closed were in Barnard, Bellows Falls, Lyndonville, Morrisville, Northfield, St. Albans, and Wilmington. In 1926, there were twelve active branches holding Sunday services and twelve practitioners, two of whom were teachers.

In the difficult years for The Mother Church central organization, known as the "Litigation Period," the Journals for 1919-1920 & 1920-1921, carried practitioner's or teacher's cards on a quarterly basis, though some chose not to have their cards in the magazine, and only Bennington, Montpelier, Morrisville, Northfield, Randolph, and Rutland were listed among the Churches and Societies. During this time there is evidence that students of Christian Science gathered in Masonic Halls, shared church buildings,

city parlors, and farm kitchens often holding both Sunday services and Sunday School.

The Green Mountain Junior College in Poultney was the first post-secondary educational institution in Vermont to have a College Organization made up of students and faculty who were Christian Scientists. They began their advertising in the 1946 Journal. This was followed in 1949 with a listing for Middlebury College, and in 1955, for the University of Vermont.

By 1954, Christian Scientists had been holding church services in all the branches listed on the Contents Page. Only in Woodstock would it be another several years before the Christian Scientists asked for official recognition by The Mother Church. Eight of the branches qualified as churches with more than enough members, a practitioner, Wednesday meetings as well as Sunday services, and a Reading Room open to the public. While several of the smaller branches had closed, the truth of the matter was the advancement in the state of transportation. There were, by the mid 1950s, a few paved roads, so that Christian Scientists in St. Albans, for example, could get to Burlington; and those in Wilmington could get to Brattleboro; and those in Northfield and Morrisville could get to Montpelier or Barre.

What Mrs. Eddy wrote on May 6, 1905, to the members of the Massachusetts Metaphysical College class applies as well to those wonderful early Vermonters:

> Watch, pray, demonstrate. Released from materialism, you shall run and not be weary, walk and not faint.

Vermonters at Pleasant View and Chestnut Hill...

We believe that at least eight Vermonters served in Mrs. Eddy's households. Among the first was Foster Eddy, M.D., C.S.D. who moved from Waterbury to Boston to help with Mrs. Eddy's publishing efforts. Mrs. Eddy kept a room for him at Pleasant View, though he stayed mostly in Boston.

We can make a stretch and say that Miss Ellen E. Cross, C.S.D., who lived in Waterford, Vermont, from the age of nine until she moved first to Syracuse and then to Baltimore -- at each location helping to establish Christian Science churches -- was a "Vermonter" who served in Mrs. Eddy's household. It was in 1903 that she was at Pleasant View twice: August 16-September 6; and October 8-November 8. Miss Cross was, after all, Vermont's first listed practitioner. [See Section 4.]

William Clark, C.S.B., of Barre, worked for a brief time as a gardener at Pleasant View. When Mrs. Eddy was preparing to make the move from Concord to Boston in 1907, she called on Laura and Byron Burt of St. Johnsbury to help with the move, and engaged Mr. Burt as her driver. Mr. Burt, who was in charge of the horses and Mrs. Eddy's driver, passed away soon after arriving at Chestnut Hill. [See Section 4.]

Frank Bowman, who with his wife Charlotte (Lottie) lived in Essex Junction where Mrs. Bowman was a listed practitioner, came to Mrs. Eddy's home in Chestnut Hill in December 1908, and remained with her until her passing on December 3, 1910. It was Mr. Bowman who drove Mrs. Eddy's carriage the one day she asked to be taken close by The Mother Church after

the Extension had been completed. Mrs. Bowman also served at Chestnut Hill as a cook. One of Mr. Bowman's co-workers at Chestnut Hill wrote in her diary about Mrs. Eddy telling Frank Bowman that, "He had given her the worst ride of her life" one early spring day.

It seems that Bowman, more used to driving in Vermont on frost-filled roads, had not realized that the snow which had covered the road in that Boston suburb in the morning would be half mush and half frozen come time for Mrs. Eddy's afternoon ride, and he had not taken off the sleigh runners to put on the wheels. The next day, having learned his lesson, Bowman not only moved from the sleigh to the carriage, but detoured around the pot holes, earning from Mrs. Eddy the statement as she was helped out of the carriage by a member of the household, "Thank you, Mr. Bowman, for the best ride of my life."

An obituary report from the Burlington Free Press of September 13, 1944, tells of the burial service for Mr. Bowman at the Essex Junction cemetery, stating that while he was a resident of Vermont he had run a general store and served on the school board in Essex Junction, then moved to Massachusetts (the years serving Mrs. Eddy), then he went on to Minneapolis where he worked for a merchandise company. Mrs. Maude C. Harrod, CS, of Burlington, officiated at the service.

And, of course, Asa Gilbert Eddy of Londonderry, Vermont, not only served in the household, but was the first practitioner to put up a sign announcing his profession to the general public.

Some of the very early workers at The Mother Church headquarters were the daughters of Mary

Waite Warren who lived first in West Georgia, then in St. Albans, and when she moved to Montpelier was among the charter members of that Society. [See Section Three.] Lucia Crisola Warren, the oldest daughter, as well as her sister, Mary Alethea Warren, worked for the Clerk of The Mother Church (William B. Johnson), and first Lucia then Alethea learned from him how to play the The Mother Church chimes. Lucia was the official chimer for thirteen years beginning in 1907. Lucia also taught a younger sister, Caroline, to chime; and the youngest sister, Winifred, served as a messenger and errand-runner at The Mother Church headquarters for some fifty years.

When Julia Bartlett came to Vermont to visit or to teach a class, she stayed always in the Warren home, but we do not know whether her visits were in St. Albans or Montpelier.

Lucia Warren worked for many years at headquarters, finally becoming the corresponding secretary for the Board of Directors. Her sister Alethea also worked in the Clerk's office, hand-writing the payroll checks and helping with the wrapping and addressing (by hand) of the first issues of *The Christian Science Monitor*.

We also can claim Emma Shipman, CSD, as a Vermonter (from Danville) even though she spent most of her adult years in the Boston area serving The Mother Church in several capacities. The following article, written by Miss Shipman, appeared in the July 26, 1900 Sentinel (page 768): We reproduce it here as confirmation that the kindly people of Vermont early embraced the teachings of Christian Science.

Books in the Running Brooks

By Emma C. Shipman

Among the many brooks which flow into one of the larger rivers in the White Mountains is one which I watched for several summers.

When the water was high in the little brook it made a very pleasing picture, gurgling gleefully over the shining stones and flowing swiftly out into the river, carrying off its own debris and also much from the larger stream that was inclined to pile up near its outlet.

After the hot summer sun had melted all the snow from the mountain peaks and dried up the rivulets that fed the little brook, it presented a different picture. Not only was it unable to get rid of its own debris, but that from the river would be borne in upon it till one could hardly see its waters and the former happy brooklet was an unsightly and almost stagnant pool.

Occasionally, children would clear the accumulated rubbish from the outlet and try to arrange stones near the mouth of the brook to keep out the river's flotage, but this gave it a better appearance only for the day. The one real remedy was for it to become a rapidly flowing stream.

This illustrated to me a helpful lesson in Christian Science. If we would send out the swift, sparkling currents of purity, we must be fed by pure Truth and take in plenty of it. Then this current of Truth and Love will sweep the error out of our own thought and help to carry off much that is floating in the larger stream of mortal mind, thereby blessing the world.

Christian Science

Let us be so filled with the "river of the water of life" that thought cannot lose its activity under the seeming heat of error, but we shall journey on more joyfully, knowing our source is inexhaustless Life and Love.

In the words of our beloved Leader to the White Mountain Church [See Misc. 184-186.], "The rocks, rills, mountains, meadows, fountains, and forests of our native state should be prophetic of the finger Divine that writes in living character their lessons on our lives."

SECTION TWO
VERMONT
AT THE TURN-
OF-THE-CENTURY

The More Things Change,
    the More They Stay the Same

Moving by Rail

Working

Playing

In God We Trust

Taxes, Women, and Reforms

 Christian Science

People of the Dawnland

Education and Medication

The End of an Era

Vermont

at the

Turn-of-the-Century

The More Things Change, the More They Stay the Same

Uncovering the Vermont that existed at the turn-of-the-century is a bit like looking in a mirror and finding you haven't changed as much as you'd believed. One comes away humbled by the slow pace of human learning and inattention to history, but with a connection to the past, more a sense of deja vu.

Vermont, from approximately 1880 to 1920, bustled with commerce, wrestled with rapid growth, and occasionally with equally rapid decline; fretted over a period of massive emigration; invited and then drew back from a wide spectrum of immigration, and built railroads, churches, schools, libraries, and hospitals -- activities -- with the notable exception of

railroad building -- that could well describe the most recent 40 years of its existence.

At the turn of the century, Vermont's web of commerce reached beyond its borders and, in some industries, beyond the nation. In the winter of 1887-88, hardwood logs cut in Victory, Vermont -- then the site of one of the Northeast's earliest logging and lumbering operations -- were shipped to Montreal by rail and from there by boat to South Korea, to be made into piano cabinets (which, no doubt, were then shipped to the United States and other countries). The "global marketplace may be a new phrase; for Vermont, it is not a new idea.

And, there is a modern-day echo to be heard in the criticism of Vermont state government by Orion B. Barber of Arlington, state auditor of accounts from 1898 to 1902, for its tendency to some increase in nearly every line of the state expenses -- in some instances warranted and in others unwarranted. Vermont government expenditures in 1840 were $90,000; by 1904, they had reached $1.2 million. Orion probably had a point.

In a 1900 report, the state of education and its practitioners were broadly criticized in resoundingly familiar terms: urban schools were overcrowded, teachers poorly prepared, attendance low in many schools, and students were not learning grammar. As the report noted, "Parsing is almost a lost art, and the uses of the parts of speech, and the relations of the parts of a sentence to each other, have lost their significance in great measure, and are only dimly seen."

Women's issues, then as now, stimulated debate and controversy, although then, the focus was

primarily on suffrage. For Vermont's women it was a long battle; Vermont was the last state (in 1917) to grant women the right to vote. Meanwhile, men continued to run almost every aspect of the state. The 36th annual report of the City of Burlington (1900) by Matthew H. Buckham lists the board members, aldermen, assessors, water commissioners, and members of the fire and police departments. The list is all male. The same report totals 73 teachers, 67 of whom are female. It also notes for that year some 173 marriages; 545 births; and 346 deaths. The record shows the youngest mother was 15; the oldest, 48.

Vermont's interest in cultural events and entertainments also has early roots. Vermont in 1887 had everything from the Lake Champlain Yacht Club, where elite citizens such as W. Seward Webb of Shelburne and his New York society friends practiced four-in-hand coaching, to home-grown baseball teams, to the ubiquitous fairs with their farm-centered competitions, parades, and visiting circus troupes.

Vermont's reputation for environmentalism has some historical basis in this period, as well. According to J. Kevin Graffagnino in *Vermont in the Victorian Era*, by the 1890s, the public and private wildlife programs were beginning to work effectively in Vermont, which, by then, had established two fish hatcheries. In 1897, open season on deer killing lasted one month; by 1900, it had been reduced to ten days.

Above all, Vermonters represented a patchwork-quilt of religions; they were: Congregationalists, Episcopalians, Baptists, Quakers, Universalists, Methodists, Presbyterians, Unitarians, Catholics, Christian Scientists, Seventh Day Adventists, Advent Christians, Jews, and Mormons.

Almost no history of this period, however, reports on the lives, commerce, schooling, or religious practices of Vermont's Native American population, reflecting a pervasive cultural and historical ignorance not much different from today. A longstanding tenet of Vermont's history is denial of Indian presence in the region before European settlements. Native Americans, however, are indeed indigenous to Vermont and have never relinquished title to their lands here, notes historian Colin Calloway. The 1890 census listed 34 civilized Indians among Vermont's then 332,422 people, civilized being the term applied to Indians living off reservations.

Moving by Rail

The period of 1840 to 1910 was the heyday of railroad building in this country. Vermont was quick to catch the fever, and railroads became the linchpin of the state's development. By the end of this era, their dominance faded into reluctant partnership with newer forms of transport, which eventually claimed sovereignty.

The influence of the railroad, if brief, was dramatic. A trip that was once a week's journey by oxcart, or two days by stage, came to be measured in hours. Areas that were self-sufficient no longer had to rely on their own production and could specialize in economic pursuits best suited to their location. Isolated communities opened up and new communities grew

up, including all of Vermont's major cities. As reported in Vol. I of *Railroads of Vermont*, the railroads opened the way for early commerce to flow . . . Behind the laboring locomotive came the farmer, the merchant, the millwright, the stone cutter, and all the adventurous company who built the towns, cut the hay, and filled the woods with the sound of the biting ax. For those living along the Lake Champlain shoreline, a choice could be made between traveling by boat or by rail.

Railroads and the mills they served existed symbiontically, and as either went, so went Vermont. The town of Gallup Mills' business directory in 1895 listed a millinery and dressmaking shop, a sawmill, a doctor, Methodist and Catholic Churches, and a Good Templars Lodge. There were 50 families in the town. Two miles north, Stevens Mill had 45 families. The Methodists worshiped in the schoolhouse, and the Catholic ceremony was conducted by a priest who traveled from St. Johnsbury every three weeks. Nine years later, the local mills closed, the villages were abandoned, and the houses carted away.

Many rail lines were built for exclusive reasons -- most often to serve quarries or lumbering operations, as was the 11-mile Victory Branch that helped debut the Korean pianos. A unique example was the Manchester, Dorset and Granville Railroad, a line that was built to build the New York Public Library. The Plateau Quarry in South Dorset was inactive in 1900 when the order for marble came to a local company. Plateau had just the right kind of marble, and so, the company reopened the quarry and, by 1902, built a railroad to serve it; the library was completed in 1911. Plateau marble also was shipped to Cambridge, Massachusetts, where it graces the annex of Harvard's Medical College.

The railroads also opened borders, carried innovation from other states, and allowed Vermonters to travel -- and even leave for good, as many did in this era, seeking employment and a better life. Between 1850 and 1900, two of every five Vermonters left the state. Vermont historian, Charles Morrissey, says, "No other state in the nation was losing such a large proportion of its people." Many of those who stayed extended their horizons through commuter travel. The Montpelier and Wells River Railroad offered passenger service with daily round trips by a mailtrain, an express, and an accommodation train with a through parlor car to Boston, a trip that became very popular. One train left Montpelier at 8 a.m. and arrived in Boston at 4:45 p.m. Another left Boston at 1 p.m. and arrived in Montpelier at 8:35 P.M. [Either this accommodation was not in service when Mrs. Eddy came from Boston to Barton in 1882, or, quite possibly, she took three days in order to visit along the way with friends and relatives.]

Rail trips, even more local ones, were an adventure unto themselves. Constance Votey, in a marvelous reminiscence written when she was 90, describes her family's annual move from Burlington to Greensboro, where they had a summer home at Aspenhurst, a settlement established around the time of her birth, in 1893. Constance, one of four daughters of Josiah William Votey, dean of the Engineering College at the University of Vermont (and for whom the present engineering building is named), remembers that the family shipped their trunks and piano! two weeks before the actual journey, which began at 7 a.m. in a surrey with fringe, loaded with mother, father, the girls, the cat, dog, and canary, and an assortment of luggage, tennis rackets, and golf clubs. At the railroad depot, all was unloaded and reloaded on the train, the

smell of which Constance recalls as a mixture of dusty red plush seats, coal smoke, sweaty humans, peanuts, and orange peels. The windows were unscreened, she says, and we had a choice of hazards: suffocation with the windows closed or a hot cinder in the eye from the engine's smokestack. On the journey, the girls played the animal game, awarding one point for spotting a cow, two for a sheep (then numerous) five for a horse, ten for an ox (still in use for heavy hauling), and 25 for a wild animal.

At Cambridge Junction, the group off-loaded and re-embarked on a train for East Hardwick. Once, mother Votey got left behind, surrounded by tennis rackets and cases. The train had ambled to Jeffersonville, but the conductor backed it all the way to Cambridge Junction to collect mother and her goods. "Amtrak will never be like that," comments Constance.

Next stop was Morrisville, for lunch, where one year, says Constance, "My dog escaped from the baggage car and high-tailed it down the tracks toward Burlington." The train waited until the dog was caught -- The idea of speed had not then penetrated so deeply into American lives.

They reached East Hardwick in late afternoon and were met with a hayrack and a 2-seater for the folks. On the long hills, they all got out and walked to save the horses.

The railroads also brought immigrants, both to build the lines, and to work in the industries supporting and supported by the lines. The granite quarries of Barre brought Italian and Scottish stone workers in the 1880s and 1890s. Before them, the Irish had been the major immigrant group, come to build the rails and toil

in factories and still finding time to become a noteworthy factor in the Democratic Party. French Canadians worked in textile factories, quarries, lumber camps, and on farms. They developed French-speaking schools and social organizations and remained fairly insular. By 1900, the Vermont census recorded 44,747 foreign-born residents. The mutual distrust of one group for another and the discrimination they all experienced at the hands of native Vermonters resonates for many still in today's immigrant experience.

Working

Not all of Vermont was farms, quarries, and lumber mills. Factories were on the rise as well and becoming a more important factor than agriculture. Burlington was the top industrial city, with Barre and Rutland a distant second and third. In 1900, there were only two carding mills left and factories (frequently called mills) had taken over, with 1,938 factories and 28,000 workers. Lumbering had about 6,000 workers; paper, woolen, and cotton mills (factories) accounted for the rest. Despite the eventual demise of the woolen and cotton mills, Winooski remained the textile center of Vermont until the American Woolen Mill closed operations in 1956.

Orange County had a long-active copper industry, around which Ely (named for Ely Goddard who controlled the Vermont Copper Mining Co.) grew

and later was the site of a miners' riot when the mine closed in the 1890s.

By 1884, the insurance industry was well-established in Montpelier with three companies: Vermont Mutual, National Life, and Union Mutual. The Montpelier Carriage Co. turned out children's carriages, sleds, sleighs, and rocking chairs. In 1886, electric lights lined Montpelier's State Street, which, by 1900, was home to three banks. The city's population (6,266), had increased 171 percent since 1850.

By 1896, Grand Isle County was increasingly devoted to commercial apple growing, producing a crop of 40,000 apples in a wide variety: Northern Spy, Baldwin, Rhode Island Greening, Fameuse, Tallman Sweet, Golden Russet, Ben Davis, and Yellow Bellflower. Greenings sold for $3 a barrel and Fameuse for $1.90 a barrel.

The U.S. production of maple syrup reached 50 million pounds in 1889, with Vermont holding a strong lead over New York State and Canada.

Before the railroad era, Merino sheep covered Vermont, and much land had been cleared for their grazing, which reached its peak in the 1830s. The decline of sheep raising was due primarily to the lowering of tariffs and to competition from the west, which had much more land to devote to sheep. In 1880, the census recorded that Vermont had 429,870 sheep (and 332,286 people and 217,033 cows). By 1910, only 118,551 sheep remained (with a modest growth to 355,956 people and 265,483 cows - note: not more cows than people!).

Playing

Leisure was a reality for many people, even those who worked hard six days a week. People enjoyed ice skating, snowshoeing, tobogganing, or hockey in the winter months, swimming, hiking, and boat and rail rides in the summer. Most towns had bands, and visiting lecturers spoke on everything from temperance to the wonders of Hindustan, to Arctic explorations. The nation's first Boy Scout Troop was founded in Barre in 1911. The Grange, Eagles, Elks, Freemasons, Odd Fellows, Red Men, Ancient Order of Hibernians, Grand Templars, and Knights of Pythias were adult male bastions, as were the Owl Club in St. Albans, The Algonquin in Burlington, the Apollo in Montpelier, the Mystic in St. Johnsbury, and many more.

For those with more time and more money, there were the aforementioned Lake Champlain Yacht Club, the Qaubanakee Golf Club for Golf and Tennis, and numerous other golf clubs. Baseball was very popular in most towns; the 1893 University of Vermont team finished second in the Chicago World's Fair tournament.

By 1900, Vermonters had made the connection between recreation and tourism, with railroads often leading the way. Vermont had numerous spas with mineral springs, many with hotels; there was at least one amusement venue, Barber Park, complete with theater (high class vaudeville between acts), at the end of the Bellows Falls and Saxtons River Street Railway.

In 1895, New York capitalists built a casino and a resort, Camp Comfort, just outside Bennington,

served by the Bennington and Glastenbury railroad. The round trip to the resort was 10 cents, and 15 cents to a new hotel, the Glastenbury Inn, where dinner was 75 cents. The venture was short-lived, as the line was washed away in 1898 and the inn destroyed by fire.

Many of the state's libraries were built in this period, including the Kellogg-Hubbard in Montpelier, and reading joined the ranks of leisure as well as education. "Household," a monthly journal devoted to the interests of the American housewife, was published by George Crowell in Brattleboro. Its subjects covered everything from management of horses to human hygiene. It was filled with lengthy advice on gardening, parenting, needlework, and cooking. (A cheap dinner: Buy a knuckle of veal and have the bone sawed apart two or three times. Put into cold water over the fire... early next morning ... now put in the corn.) And fiction: "A Day By the Mississippi River -- It was a dark, cloudy evening in September when . . . " And ads for waved hair, Diamond dyes, Royal Baking Powder, and the books of Longfellow, Emerson, and Whittier.

In all, Vermonters were an industrious group who, as today, seemed to wield influence well beyond their state. In the early 20th century, as *Vermont in the Victorian Age* boasts: More native Vermonters were listed in *Who's Who*, in proportion to state population, than from any other state, exceeding the national average by four to one.

In God We Trust

By 1910, Christian Science churches had been established in St. Johnsbury, Montpelier and Barre, Randolph, Rutland, Burlington/Essex Junction, Newport, Brattleboro, Bennington, St. Albans, all of which were served by at least one rail line.

Springfield boasted a Russian orthodox church, founded by immigrants who came from an area between Minsk, Russia and Vilna, Poland, to work in local machine shops.

St. Joseph's, in Burlington, was the first French Catholic parish in the nation (est. 1850), and, as noted before, Catholic and numerous other Christian sects held sway throughout the state.

The state's first synagogue was built in Burlington, in 1885, by Russian and Polish Jews, and there were small Jewish communities in Poultney, West Rutland, Montpelier, and St. Albans.

Taxes, Women, and Reforms

In 1892, the state authorized taxes for road repair and formed the Vermont League for Good Roads (still in existence) so farmers could get their produce to market more quickly.

The legislature was slower to recognize the rights of women. By 1880, Vermont was the only state in New

Vermont

England without an active suffrage association. However, there was suffrage activity, and it gradually grew strong, with help from more sophisticated and experienced organizers in other states. Between 1888 and 1917, a bill granting women the vote passed one branch of the legislature only to be defeated in the other, possibly an effort by the legislators to keep the women's movement off-balance.

In 1880, the Vermont legislature passed a bill allowing women to vote in local school district meetings, and, in 1917, Vermont became the first state in New England to permit women to vote in municipal elections. In 1919, the legislature passed a bill allowing women the vote in presidential elections, but Governor Percival C. Clement called it unconstitutional and vetoed it. The following year, he refused to call a special session of the legislature to ratify the 19th amendment to the U.S. constitution, and the distinction of being the 36th (and last) state to ratify it was lost to Vermont. On August 26, 1920, Tennessee ratified the amendment, and women's suffrage became the law of the land.

Vermont also was the last state to have a child labor law (in 1867), however weak. In 1897, for example, a ten-year-old child could work ten hours a day if she/he had attended 20 weeks of school the previous year; a fifteen-year-old could work unlimited hours.

People of the Dawnland

Abenaki translates as people of the Dawnland or, simply, easterners. The Abenaki had viable settlements in New England and Canada and were a sovereign people when the French first made contact with them. New England Indians were making maple syrup long before the colonists arrived. Using a tomahawk, they cut a long slanting gash in the bark and then cut a notch for a chip along which the sap could flow into a birch bark receptacle. It was then boiled in a kettle to make syrup. The Coosus, Pennacook, Penobscot, Pocumtuc, and Sokoki, related tribes, also are indigenous to Vermont and shared Abenaki culture and the Algonquian language. The Abenaki, deeply devout people, exhibited extraordinary artistry in crafts, particularly in basketry and beading.

Although Abenaki men had attended Dartmouth College as early as 1773, and although Vermont (Missisquoi) Abenaki had helped the American colonists in the War of 1812, they remained invisible people to the settlers of Vermont, who adopted the term Native Vermonters for themselves. (In the category some things never change, the 1960 census listed 57 Indians as living in Vermont.)

The Abenaki's Seven Nations land claim was presented to the Vermont legislature at least three times between 1800 and 1896 and denied all three times. In 1900, the United States rescinded the right of St. Francis Abenaki (in Montreal) to cross the border without paying duty on their basketry, a source of both pride and income for the tribe.

Vermont

Many of Vermont's place names are from Native American languages, among them Monadnock Mountain in Lemington (mountain which sticks up like an island); Winooski (onion); Passumpsic River (clear, sandy bottom) Okemo (a louse in Abenaki; a chieftain in Chippewa); and Jamaica Town (Natic for beaver).

In this era, one briefly heralded Native American from New England was Louis Francis Sackalexis, a member of the Penobscot, who played professional baseball from 1897 to 1899 for the Cleveland Spiders. Sackalexis died young, and the team renamed itself the Cleveland Indians, in his honor.

Education and Medication

Although the State Normal School at Castleton was founded in 1787 and, in 1889, tuition was only six dollars for the twenty-week quarter, most Vermont teachers did not attend the preparatory training. Of the seventy-three teachers listed in the Burlington 1900 report, three had attended normal schools (only two had graduated), and only eleven were college graduates. But then, many of Vermont's children did not show up in their classrooms, either. Contemporary estimates were that at least two-fifths of Vermont's children did not go to school at all, the worst state attendance percentage in New England. Rural schools frequently had fewer than a total of fifteen children from grades one through eight, although urban schools sometimes had one-to-sixty teacher-student ratios.

In 1892, schools were consolidated, reducing their numbers by 90 percent; the school year was lengthened; textbooks were now provided free; and towns with more than 2,500 people were required to establish high schools.

Most of the state's major hospitals were built in this era, with Mary Fletcher, in Burlington, the first, in 1876; St. Albans Hospital in 1888; Rutland Hospital in 1892; Fanny Allen, in Winooski, in 1894; St. Johnsbury Hospital, in 1895; Proctor in 1896; Brattleboro Memorial in 1904; and Springfield in 1914. (The Medical Department at the University of Vermont (UVM) was organized in 1807.)

Treatment may not have been high-tech, but it carried a more reasonable price tag than does today's service. In 1900, Mary Fletcher Hospital treated 1,386 people, 863 in-patients and 523 out-patients. Only 157 of them paid the regular rate of $10 per week; 541 were admitted free of charge, and all out-patients were free. There was an out-patient clinic for eye, ear, and throat cases every Tuesday and Friday from 4 to 6 P.M.

The End of an Era

Vermont's railroad era ended with a whimper, a victim of the technology it had modeled as well as the technological visions it inspired.

Toward the end of the 19th century, many cities and towns had added street railways, essentially

small-circuit, passenger and freight services, many of which connected to the larger rail service. Some were horse drawn, but increasingly they became electric. The Barre and Montpelier Traction Power Co. is a good example. It ran between the two cities, a 7.7 mile journey, as well as within each city. According to *Railroads of Vermont, A Pictorial History*, it gave the three railroads in those communities serious competition, as did others in their communities, including the Bellows Falls and Saxtons River Street Railway, the Bennington Electric Railway, and the Burlington Traction Co.

Not all citizens embraced the change. Brattleboro's street railroad had a stellar opponent in Rudyard Kipling, who had married a native. Perhaps he was thinking of the peace and quiet he needed to write *Captains Courageous* and the first and second *Jungle Books*, when he railed against the line, citing permanent disfigurement of the streets and violent death or mutilation of human beings. Despite Kipling's dramatic opposition, the line was built, in 1895. In the period of 1909 to 1911, it carried 400,000 passengers. Its demise came one day in 1923, and buses took over the routes the next day.

The combustion engine, powering buses, trucks, and automobiles, overtook the railroads functions in Vermont as well as throughout the country. At least one Vermonter went down in the history books for his fanatical devotion to the horseless carriage. In 1903, Dr. H. Nelson Jackson, a Vermonter visiting in San Francisco, accepted a wager that the motor car could not be driven across country. He left San Francisco in May in a Winton car, christened "The Vermont," and for two months and nine days, he and his co-driver battled bad roads, no roads, breakdowns, and flat tires, before

arriving in New York City. He later returned to Vermont in the same car.

To end this essay on a delightful note, we discovered an October 3, 1903, news dispatch in "Contrary Country" which reported that: "Dr. H. N. Jackson, first man to cross the continent in an automobile, was arrested in Burlington, Vermont, and fined for driving the machine more than six miles an hour."

Leona Griffin
Winooski, Vermont

Vermont

Bibliography

The Abenaki
(Indians of North America Series)
Colin G. Calloway
Chelsea House Press
New York and Philadelphia 1989

Constance Votey: Moments in a Life,
Reflections on an Era
Edited by Alan B. Howes
Greensboro Historical Society
Greensboro, Vt. 1995

Contrary County:
A Chronicle of Vermont
Ralph Nading Hill
Shelburne Museum
Shelburne, Vt. 1950

Dawnland Encounters:
Indians and Europeans in Northern New England
Colin G. Calloway
University Press of New England
Hanover, N.H. 1991

A History of the Abenaki People
Ken Pierce
UVM Instructional Development Center
Burlington 1977

"Household"
A monthly journal devoted to the interests of the American housewife
Vol. xvi
George Crowell
Brattleboro, Vt. 1883

In a State of Nature
Readings in Vermont History
H. Nicholas Muller and Samuel B. Hand
Vermont Historical Society
Montpelier, Vt. 1982

One Half the People: The Fight for Women's Suffrage
Anne Fern Scott and Andrew Mackay Scott
University of Illinois Press
Urbana, Ill. 1975

Railroads of Vermont, Volume I
Robert C. Jones
New England Press
Shelburne, Vt. 1993

Railroads of Vermont
A Pictorial
Robert C. Jones
New England Press
Shelburne, Vt. 1994

36th Annual Report of the City of Burlington, Vermont
Matthew H. Buckham
Burlington, Vt. 1900

Vermont

Time and Change in Vermont
A Human Geography
Harold A. Meeks
The Globe Pequot Press
Chester, Conn. 1986

Vermont, A History
Charles T. Morrissey
W.W. Norton & Co., Inc.
1981

Vermont in the Victorian Age
Continuity and Change in the Green Mountain State
1850-1900
J. Kevin Graffagnino
Vermont Heritage Press and Shelburne Museum
Bennington and Shelburne, Vt. 1985

Vermont Under Four Flags
A History of the Green Mountain State 1635-1975
Percy H. Merrill

The Victory Branch Railroad of Vermont
Gordon E. Hopper
Heinberger House Publishing Co.
River Forest, Ill. 1989

Christian Science

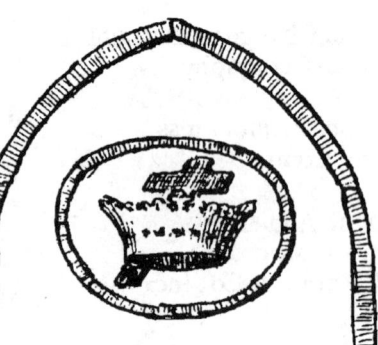

The sick need you and you can do great good by healing. The Cause needs healers a million times more than teachers. The best healer is the best Scientist and will take the place that God has for all to take.

Mary Baker Eddy
[Journal Vol. 114, No. 9]

SECTION THREE
BRANCH BY BRANCH

St. Johnsbury, 1886

Montpelier, 1888

Randolph, 1890

Barre, 1894

Rutland, 1894

Burlington, 1896

Newport, 1898

Brattleboro, 1898

Bennington, 1900

St. Albans, 1904-1913

Bellows Falls, 1906-1965

Lyndonville, 1907-1975

Springfield/Chester, 1908

Wilmington, 1910-1920

Barnard, 1911-1915

Northfield, 1918-1951

Morrisville, 1919-1942

Middlebury, 1941

Poultney, 1951

Woodstock, 1961

Christian Science

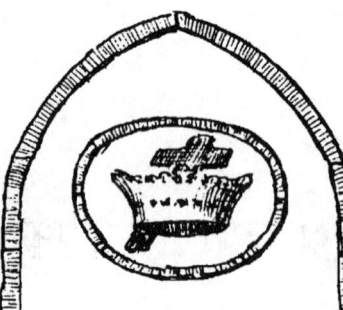

...less teaching and more healing is <u>best for our Cause</u> and for the students; fewer reports of new churches and more testimonials of our cures, argue more for the progress of Christian Science.

Mary Baker Eddy
[Journal Vol. 114, No.9]

Branch by Branch

"How beautiful upon the mountains are the feet of him that bringeth good tidings...that saith unto Zion, Thy God reigneth!" Surely, the Word that is God must at some time find utterance and acceptance throughout the earth, for he that soweth shall reap.

Mary Baker Eddy

St. Johnsbury, 1886

In 1898 when First Church of Christ, Scientist, St. Johnsbury offered the first branch-sponsored public lecture on Christian Science in Vermont, there was a great deal of healing work going on in the area. In 1898, there were more than sixteen in the congregation, services every Sunday including a Sunday School, mid-week testimony meetings, and an active Reading Room. In this year, St. Johnsbury Society became the state's third -- after Barre and Burlington -- recognized branch. George P. Moore was listed in the Journal as First Reader in 1898. They held that first public meeting

Christian Science

at 10.45 A.M. at No. 33 Pearl Street at the home of Mrs. and Mrs. Luman Ladd.

The first six members were three couples: Luman A. and Nellie Green Ladd; Byron S. and Laura W. Burt; George P. and Harriett J. Moore. Mr. and Mrs. Burt were called to Pleasant View to serve Mrs. Eddy at the time she was making her move from Concord to Chestnut Hill in Boston. [See Section Four.]

Several practitioners were active in the area before 1902. Mr. and Mrs. Wm. J. Moore were listed in the Journal only in 1892-1894. Their address was 33 Pearl Street, same as that of Mr. and Mrs. Ladd in 1898. Mrs. Burt had her card in the Journal beginning in November 1893, as did Mrs. Elsie A. Flood who lived a few miles south in McIndoe Falls. Harriet J. Moore joined the St. Johnsbury Church in 1897 and was listed in the 1901 Journal. Katherine Puffer, who sometime before 1907 was a listed practitioner, joined St. Johnsbury Church in 1899. Jessie H. Carrick began her listing in 1902. [See Section Four.]

In 1914, Katherine Puffer and Elsie A. Flood were no longer listed in Vermont, but Mrs. Burt and Mrs. Harriet Moore were, and had been joined by Ida Fuller Moore. That same year, Ellis Walker Moore was the First Reader. In 1918, Ida Fuller Moore was the First Reader.

In January, 1901, the church members showed how little intimidated they were by a Vermont winter by having a public lecture given by Irving C. Tomlinson. They gave a second lecture that year on October 1, 1901. The following report appeared in the October 24, 1901 Sentinel (p. 118), and was a reprint

St. Johnsbury

from the local newspaper, the St. Johnsbury Caledonian:

>A good sized and representative audience gathered in Music Hall last Tuesday evening (October 1) to listen to the lecture on Christian Science by Hon. William G. Ewing of Chicago. In the gathering were many from the surrounding towns, some of whom had come many miles to hear this lecture.
>
>Judge Ewing was introduced by George P. Moore, and spoke without notes in an interesting and logical manner. His address was very religious in tone and followed closely the teachings of Christ. The audience paid him excellent attention and seemed deeply interested in his lecture. He gave a statement of the belief of Christian Scientists, and said the race was in bondage to the old-time customs and beliefs of our ancestors, but gradually the human race was being freed from these doctrines that fettered us.
>
>In the course of his lecture he paid warm tribute to Mrs. Mary Baker Eddy, and to all the noble women of the past and present age, beginning with the mother of Christ. After the lecture Christian Science literature was distributed at the door.

The St. Johnsbury Church continued the practice of giving a fall lecture and invited Judge Ewing to be their speaker on October 28, 1902. He was introduced by the Honorable Elisha May. Two days later, Judge Ewing lectured in Brattleboro, a six or seven hour train ride south.

The church services were first held in two different private homes, then in three public buildings before 1918 when the members purchased and renovated an unoccupied Baptist church on Main

Street. By 1933 they had completed the remodeling of the upstairs auditorium, and because the branch was free of indebtedness they were able to dedicate the building and hold a public lecture the same afternoon. The Hon. William E. Brown of Los Angeles, California, was the speaker.

Several members of the St. Johnsbury branch had their testimonies published in the Journal and Sentinel. [See Section Four.] We have learned a little bit about some of them. Angeline Towle, whose testimony was published in the Journal in the July 1910 issue, joined The Mother Church in 1905, with Katherine Puffer endorsing her application and Emma Shipman as her countersigner. Mrs. Maude A. May, who lived in West Concord, joined The Mother Church in 1911, her application being endorsed by George Moore of St. Johnsbury. The Pecks (Charles and May), whose testimonies were chosen by Mrs. Eddy to be in "Fruitage" in the textbook, both joined The Mother Church in 1902, their applications having been endorsed by George Moore and countersigned by Ira Knapp. Mr. Peck was listed as the First Reader in St. Johnsbury in 1905; he passed away in 1930, Mrs. Peck in 1937, both having served in First Church of Christ, Scientist, St. Johnsbury since 1902.

Mr. Peck's testimony originally appeared in the March, 1907 Journal. The Sentinel for 1900 had three testimonies by women living near St. Johnsbury. Mrs. Christina A. MacJuer of Waterford, was in the February 8, issue, Mrs. Seth T. Moulton, also of Waterford, was in the May 31, issue, and Mrs. Maude A. May of West Concord, was in the June 28, issue. [See Section Four.]

Mrs. May continued writing for the Sentinel. Her further articles appeared in 1919, 1922, 1923, and 1937.

St. Johnsbury

We reprint here, first Mrs. May's testimony and next that of Mrs. Moulton:

In the fall of 1899 I gave birth to a baby girl. When she was four weeks old, I brought upon myself, by being too ambitious for my strength, a female trouble, a very uncommon and severe one. My strength entirely left me. I could sit up but a few hours at a time, and my suffering at times was intense. This thought was uppermost in my mind and I could not dismiss it. Why did this trouble come upon me? I had planned to take such comfort with my baby and had tried to be careful lest I should exert myself too much, and, like Job, the thing I greatly feared had come upon me. I was most miserable in mind and body. I knew it had healed my mother of many ills, among which was this same trouble, after doctors, medicine, and the hospital had failed to relieve her. It was pronounced by all to be a very uncommon and peculiar weakness, and they could not seem to reach it. I knew from her experience that I had no hope in material means, and was ready for Christian Science.

One day I was complaining that I must be an invalid all the rest of my life, when my mother said, "No; you need not be like this all your life. There is a cure-all, why don't you write to Mrs. D. for treatment" I answered that I had thought of it, but was not quite ready to mention it to my husband. Though he did not oppose Christian Science, yet he seemed to be of the opinion that it was more for people who did not have much the trouble with them, than for a severe sickness or organic trouble. I felt that he would want me to go through the category of patent medicines for female trouble first, and then try Christian Science if they failed to effect a cure. Imagine my surprise when that very evening as he was reading the testimonials in the *Sentinel*, he looked up and asked, "Why don't you try Christian

Christian Science

Science? Perhaps it would help you." Surely the spirit of Love moved him to speak.

I wrote to a healer the next day, and she took up my case. After I sent the letter my mother came in bringing "Science and Health with Key to the Scriptures," by Mary Baker G. Eddy, for me to read. I remember thinking, "Oh, if I could only be healed without reading that book!" for I could not understand it enough to keep my mind on it. But she left it, and I opened to page 415 and read, "Never tell the sick they have more courage than strength. Tell them, rather, that their strength is in proportion to their courage." That whole paragraph seemed to apply to me and sounded so different from anything I had previously read in the book. I read it over and over and kept the book near me after then, and read constantly. My healer worked lovingly and faithfully for me for eight or nine weeks, and to-day I am in better health than I have been for years. I am perfectly well.

My healing was very slow and for the benefit of those who expect the healing to come quickly I would like to relate some of my experiences while under treatment. I expected to be healed at once, and often wondered why it was so slow when I had turned to God first, without trying material remedies, and had so much faith in Him. In a few days I was much stronger, could sit up longer, stand on my feet longer, and in a week walked out on the street. The bodily suffering ceased almost entirely, causing me inconvenience only at times. The difficulty was not wholly removed though I was gaining in strength all the time. I kept worrying because it did not yield entirely, and thought about it all the time, until I had melancholia I was almost insane; I certainly was deranged at times I believe. Nobody can know what I suffered. I would sit for hours and cry, scream so I could be heard all over

St. Johnsbury

the house, upstairs and down, and I used to think I would write the Christian Science Publishing Society to print nothing but testimonials of slow healing; the others seemed to discourage me. But the healer was preparing the ground and sowing the good seed and this trouble was overcome, but not for several weeks.

Several other troubles yielded during the time, but the first trouble did not give up entirely. It occurred to me that possibly I was depending too much on the healer and ought to work out my own salvation. I accordingly stopped treatment and began to help myself, and now I am fully realizing my birthright -- health and strength. The completion of my cure has been so gradual that I cannot say when it occurred. I kept improving and forgetting myself until now I am "every whit whole." It was about six months that I was in error, but praise be to God, I am not an "invalid for life." I have planted, Apollos watered, but God gave the increase. No one can convince me that Christian Science did not heal me, and to Mrs. Eddy and the dear woman who helped me to find the light, I owe a debt of gratitude that can be paid in no better way than by daily striving to live the Christian life they are living.

Mrs. Maude A. May, West Concord, Vt.

Sentinel May 31, 1900

I deem it a great pleasure to testify to the harmony Christian Science has brought into my life. About two years ago I was stricken with paralysis of the right side. I was well nigh helpless and no words can express the gloom and darkness that settled on my mind. I longed to die, for that was the only way that I could see out of it all....and then it was that one of my kind neighbors,

with her heart full of love and sympathy for me, called one day and wished me to try Christian Science. I told her I had no faith in it, but would try anything.

I commenced reading "Science and Health with Key to the Scriptures." I did not understand it much at first, but by the first few treatments I was cured of dyspepsia, from which I had suffered all my life, and as I read on, the dark clouds began to lift. The Truth that makes free began to dawn, but I had many despondent hours and some days would resolve not to read the book any more; but I could not leave it, and as I read on the light would come.

The kind and loving words of my healer, the many promises she brought me from the Bible, and the light thrown upon it by Science and Health led me out of this wilderness of gloom and helplessness into green pasture where living waters are ever flowing out from the throne of God. Instead of death I have found Life eternal and always harmonious. Instead of gloom and darkness, I have found joy and light....

The Bible is a new book to me. I never could understand it very well and did not like to read it until I read Science and Health. Truly it is a key to the Scriptures, and it has unlocked for me many treasures. The world is fast finding out what a great blessing Mrs. Eddy has given to it in this book, Science and Health.... I never weary searching for Truth in the Bible and Science and Health, and my one desire is that I may have a better understanding of what these books teach and so live that I may be able to help some one else out of this wilderness of gloom and suffering.

Mrs. Seth T. Moulton, Waterford, Vt.

St. Johnsbury

The present clerk, Dorothy D. Collins tells of going with her Dad to a public concert given by the Church organist in 1936, after the purchase of a new Hammond organ. And Dorothy also provided the following special information. You'll need to get out your Hymnal to follow along.

"During the 1930s and 1940s, Mr. and Mrs. John Brewer (Edith Gaddis Brewer) summered in Peacham from Cambridge, Massachusetts, where Mr. Brewer taught at Harvard. We were most fortunate to have them attend the St. Johnsbury Church. Also summering in Peacham was Mrs. Brewer's brother and her husband, the Todd's. During that time, Mr. Brewer served as President of The Mother Church; his brother-in-law was also President of The Mother Church. [That makes three Vermonters for this honor; the other was Danville's Emma Shipman.]

"While Virgil [Dorothy's husband, who was C.O.P. from 1952-1975] and I spent a Sunday afternoon in 1946 with them they told us of their loss of their only child, a son. Mrs. Brewer was stricken with grief and decided to go alone to their cottage in Peacham during the winter months until she got her healing. At that time she received her healing and wrote two poems which are in our hymnal (#85 & #287/#408).

"The view from their cottage was tremendous, especially of the White Mountains, and in the second verse of Hymn 287 she tells that 'Faithlighted peaks of Spirit stand.' The entire poem is most descriptive of her healing."

Both Mrs. Brewer and her husband wrote metaphysical articles for the periodicals. Edith Gaddis Brewer had 12 poems and two articles published

starting in 1929. John M. Brewer wrote nine articles, all appeared in the Journal between 1934 and 1944.

Montpelier, 1888

Reverend Shipman, a Methodist Episcopalian, whose family had lived in the Montpelier area for several generations, had six children. The first to become a student of Christian Science was his semi-invalid married daughter Emily Shipman Wells who was living in New Hampshire. In 1884, a traveling saleswoman told her about the healing work of a Boston practitioner (Julia Bartlett). Her husband took her to Boston to be treated by Miss Bartlett, and within two weeks she was fully restored.

Her sister-in-law, Nell K. Shipman, who lived in Montpelier, heard of the healing and began studying Christian Science. In 1888, Nell Shipman took, as the 1946 Montpelier church report to The Mother Church Archives stated, "...Primary Class Instruction from [Mrs. Eddy] at the Massachusetts Metaphysical College, 571 Columbus Avenue, Boston, Massachusetts, and took the degree of C.S.B., her

certificate being dated October 3, 1888, and signed by Mary B.G. Eddy." [When Mrs. Shipman began teaching Christian Science she applied for the designation of "Doctor of Christian Science," and was awarded this distinction by Mrs. Eddy, thereafter using C.S.D. after her name in the *Journal* listing. See Section Four.] Mrs. Shipman's husband's sister, Mrs. Mary Dillingham, who lived we believe in Waterbury, also went through the same course of class instruction with Mrs. Eddy. Mrs. Dillingham shared a copy of *Science and Health* with a Civil War veteran, William Clark, whose healing interested many in the Montpelier and Barre area.

The church report, sent to The Mother Church Archives in 1946, continues:

> It may be of interest to know that during this [Primary Class teaching by Mary Baker Eddy] class Mrs. Shipman was completely healed of a dislocated shoulder and attendant discomfort which had been troubling her for some time before she entered the [Primary] Class.
>
> A few years later Mrs. Shipman and her husband, Charles H. Shipman, began to attend First Church of Christ, Scientist, Barre, Vermont, six miles from Montpelier, and at one time they served as Readers there. [One older member of today's Montpelier branch recalls hearing that some of the early Scientists in Montpelier walked to Barre on Sunday for the church service using the railroad tracks as their footpath.]
>
> By 1904 enough people from Montpelier were attending the Church at Barre so that it was felt a Society could be formed. Consequently October 12, 1904, Christian Science Society, Montpelier, Vermont, was formed and the following were the charter members:

Mrs. Nell K. Shipman   Phil S. Smith
Mrs. Mary Wait Warren   Mary Althea Warren
Charles H. Shipman   Mrs. Ella L. Cheney
Mrs. W.O. Standish   Mrs. Helen G. Smith
Charlotte K. Shipman

The first service was held October 16, 1904. The earliest students, as far as is known, were Mr. and Mrs. Shipman, Mrs. Standish, and Mrs. Warren. [See Section One for more information about the Warren family.] The first lecture sponsored by the Society was given by Judge Septimus H. Hanna in the Fall of 1906. [It is possible that there was an earlier lecture on July 18, 1904, given by Edward A. Kimball.]

When Nell Shipman died in 1917, the <u>Montpelier Evening Argus</u> stated in her obituary that "Mrs. Shipman was prominent in the Christian Science Society of this city, being one of the pioneer members and for three years a reader here and associated with the work nearly a quarter of a century. She was also a Christian Science practitioner and a pupil of Mary Baker Eddy."

Her husband's niece, Emma C. Shipman, was a frequent visitor to the Montpelier church, coming from Boston where she served as a practitioner, teacher, Sunday school teacher, President of The Mother Church, and author of more than thirty metaphysical articles.

The 1898 <u>Journal</u> lists Sylvester C. Hayford, C.S. under Montpelier (#7 Cummins Street), and on Wednesday he had office hours in Barre, where he was the First Reader at that time. A Mrs. T.H. Hale, C.S. was the first practitioner listed in Montpelier. She served

there for less than a year -- July 1885 through April 1886. [See Section Four.] The next, though listed in Barre, was William Clark, C.S.B. beginning in November 1894. Mr. Hayford came next in 1898, splitting his time as did Mr. Clark, between Montpelier and Barre. A year later Mr. and Mrs. Walker were listed in Barre, and in 1900, Mrs. Shipman began her advertisement in the Journal. [See Section Four.]

The May 24, 1901 issue of the newspaper, the Montpelier Argus, carried a one-sentence report which the local Committee on Publication forwarded to The Mother Church, where it is safely deposited in a catalogued box under the care of The Mother Church History Department. It reads in full: "London gossip has it that King Edward is studying Christian Science." Several weeks later, on July 17, 1901, the Montpelier Watchman, under the Barre City heading also carried a two-sentence report: "The newly organized Christian Science Society has rented rooms in the Nichols Block. The front room is used as a Reading Room."

On December 21, 1909, the Montpelier Argus reprinted the following delightful remark from The Christian Science Monitor: "It has been pointed out that the New England summer boarder industry yields more wealth than all the silver mines in America. And it looks as if the supply of pure air and fine scenery is sufficient to last for centuries." The editor followed this general reference to New England's air and scenery with: "And the very best brand is furnished in Vermont." We apologize for our provincialism, but not too vigorously.

The April 1911 Journal carried a testimony by Mrs. Josephine C. Herrick of Montpelier, who stated that she had learned of Christian Science sometime

before 1906. [See Section Four.] The Sentinel dated July 15, 1913, reported on a lecture given by Virgil O. Strickler of New York, and quoted a long introduction given by the mayor of Montpelier. The following, with minor deletions, is the text of that introduction:

> I am a member of no church and yet a friend and advocate of all churches. I respect and cherish the church because to me it is an outward symbol, variable in its structure and formularies, of an indestructible and changeless principle, or an idea planted in the heart of each man and woman by an ongoing impulse of divinity. To encourage and support the church is, therefore, one way to cooperate with God; one means of human advancement; one method of attaining individual unfoldment and contributing to the general well-being; and one process by which the individual or group of men and women may come in contact with the universal law of concord and harmony.
>
> I have only an imperfect knowledge of the teaching of Christian Science, but I have heard that it rests upon the affirmation that God is One and All; that God is Spirit, and that His followers "must worship him in spirit and in truth;" and that man is the "offspring of God" and the external universe is the manifold outpouring of His infinite oneness. This is a high concept and a wide generalization. Is it true? Is it the whole truth, and nothing but the truth? If so, it will stand the test of time and trial. We build in vain except upon the granite rock of truth, in whatever realm of research or field of action we embark.
>
> I am informed also that as a corollary to the great affirmation, God is Spirit, infinite good, the one divine presence, Christian Science denies the existence of evil as a reality and teaches that it is only a transient appearance to be dissolved by

recognition of the truth of universal good, of changeless and perfect law, and of conscious unity with the one presence, which in itself is good, is law, is harmony....

The Founder of this method of thought, growth, and worship, and her adherents, claim scientific certitude for the system if intelligently and persistently applied in personal unfoldment and in the wider affairs of social and business life. They claim, as I understand it, for their system that it is an exact Science of Christ by which each one may with certainty fulfill the ancient admonition, "Know thyself," recognize his true relation to his fellow men, and in the process of development reach a conscious union with the great source of all expression and variety. The fundamental characteristic of science is its demand for proof.... A system which does not account for and explain all the facts within the horizon of observation and knowledge is not science. Mrs. Eddy and the adherents of the system she founded admit this test of science, and claim that to follow the process and apply the rules laid down will lead to inevitable demonstration. Hence they take the third step in departure from the church in the healing of sickness and the curing of all manner of diseases. To open the "eyes of the blind" and to unstop "the ears of the deaf," "to bind up the broken-hearted" and to plant a new hope where courage has withered; and to remove pain, discomfort, and poverty, and replace them with ease, comfort, and wealth, is demonstration.

There comes one into our midst tonight to tell us of this new way. He comes with accredited authority, and if indeed, he walk in the path of science, he will speak as one having authority. I commend your attentive consideration [to] the message he brings.

By 1914, Montpelier had three practitioners, one a teacher: Mrs. Elizabeth Allen, C.S., Mrs. Nell Shipman, C.S.D., and Mrs. Phylura A. Standish, C.S. [See Section Four.] In 1914, Miss Miriam A. Kimball was the First Reader, and in 1915 and again in 1918, the First Reader was Charles A. Robie. To return to the Church report for 1946:

>A Reading Room was established November 1, 1922, and has been kept open every afternoon since except on Sundays and holidays.
>
>On May 11, 1926, the society was incorporated... and became First Church of Christ, Scientist,...and the subscribers were:
>
>Charles H. Shipman   Charles A. Robie
>Frank A. Walker   Mrs. Julia I. Flint
>Mrs. Rose F. Walker
>
>This Church was recognized by The Mother Church.
>
>To date rented quarters have been used for services and Reading Room. In March 1945, a building lot was purchased and a church will be erected as soon as conditions permit. It is worthy of note that a very substantial part of our building fund was derived from property bequeathed to this church by Charlotte Shipman Benjamin, daughter of Mrs. Nell K. Shipman, the first person in Montpelier so far as known interested in Christian Science, its first registered practitioner and its first teacher of Christian Science.
>
>Alice L. Sterling, Clerk

A later report dated October 1, 1972, and read at the dedication of the church building prominently

Montpelier

located on State Street, just two blocks from the gold-domed Capitol stated:

> The need for an improved Church [sic] auditorium and more suitable Sunday School facilities created a decision to build a new Church [sic] on the State Street site. Construction was begun in the late summer of 1971 with completion in 1972....
>
> At the first Annual Meeting of the Society in 1905 there was a discussion by the members regarding the establishing of a Sunday School. The first record of the appointment of a Sunday School Superintendent appears in the report of the Annual Meeting of October 1908....
>
> In the case of a developing organization, it is not unusual for the Reading Room to be maintained several afternoons a week in the building where Sunday services are held. That is how the Reading room developed in Montpelier. One year ago [1971] the present ground-floor location was opened, to which all are cordially invited to visit and use its research facilities.

Montpelier and Barre had the same soloist -- but not simultaneously. Dorothy Squire Farr of Waterbury sang first for Montpelier and later for Barre for more than thirty years, and tells an interesting story of why she decided to sever her ties with the local Congregational church and join the Christian Science church: "I gave birth to a son -- my second child -- and having had a very difficult labor, I had a great deal of back trouble. The organist told me we had a practitioner in our church. I took advantage of her services and was healed. I was so impressed with this healing since doctors and an osteopath had not been able to heal me that I joined the Christian Science church after much deliberation."

Christian Science

Randolph, 1890

We know that there were enough students of Christian Science in the area in 1891 to have a card in the Journal by 1896. Four years later there were enough members for the Society to become First Church of Christ, Scientist. In the 1898 Journal, Elmer and Lottie Goding, C.S. were listed in West Randolph as practitioners. [See Section Four.]

Mrs. Ida M. Green, C.S. held office hours daily except Fridays from 2-5 P.M. in nearby Rochester, as early as 1898, and a few years later, Mrs. Lizzie Messer, C.S., was a practitioner in Randolph. In 1914, Mrs. Messer was still listed in Randolph, but not Mrs. Green. That same year, Primus P. Lamson was the First Reader. The Journal for July 1916 (pp. 221-222) carried a report on the Randolph Society, telling of its beginnings. In 1918, the First Reader was Miss Mary E. Lamson. The full report follows:

> Christian Science was brought to the little mountain town of Randolph by two students who located there in the year 1891, and services were held in their home for a number of years. After a time there were about seven or eight who either had been healed or were receiving the benefits of the truth, meeting together each week, and this arrangement continued until in 1899 it seemed best to organize a church. The church was organized with seven members, and a little chapel seating about forty was then rented and fitted up for the holding of services.
>
> This little church was active in giving toward the building funds of The Mother Church, the Extension and the Publishing House, delaying purchase of its own building to this purpose. Altogether the sum of $270.59 was given, though at

this period the Randolph church had only twelve members. This money was sent at different times, and on one occasion the amount which was contributed was all the treasury contained. A good piano was the next need of the local church, and this was met by a Scientist offering a very fine one at a low figure.

The first lecture given under the auspices of this church was on Oct. 31, 1902. The next lecture was given in 1906, and since then one has been given each year, though the church has never had over fourteen members. After the second lecture was given there was a small surplus, which was sent to The Mother Church building fund. Many times, indeed, it has been proven that, as Mrs. Eddy says, "giving does not impoverish us" (Science and Health, p. 79). All have gladly helped to make the financial demonstration for the lectures, and no one has ever been asked for a contribution to any of the church activities; all has been given voluntarily, when the need was known.

A large amount of literature has been distributed and The Christian Science Monitor has been placed in the public library and in some other public institutions. This organization has also responded when there has been a call for financial aid in different parts of the field. Many members have moved away, leaving still a small band of workers, though the visiting Scientists in the tourist season help to swell the numbers in the little chapel.

The words of our beloved Leader to the White Mountain Church (My. p. 186) seem especially appropriate to the little chapel in its neighboring state: "Though neither dome nor turret tells the tale, your little song and sermon will touch the heart, point the path above the valley, up the mountain, and on to the celestial hills, echoing the Word

welling up from the infinite and swelling the loud anthem of one Father-Mother God, o'er all victorious! Reassured that He in whom dwelleth all life, health, and holiness, will supply all your needs according to His riches in glory."

But in 1921, the membership had dwindled and the church was disbanded. Yet, due to an outstanding healing in 1929 through Christian Science treatment of a well-known member of the community, Jennie S. Allen, which was acknowledged by two local highly-respected physicians, a handful of Scientists began meeting in Jennie Allen's home. In 1932, the Randolph Society was once again a recognized branch. [Note: Ramona Allen Dewey, currently president of the Randolph Society, added a personal note to the church report. She, and her sister, Ruth Allen, are granddaughters of Jennie Slack Allen.]

As was the case in branch after branch, the majority of working members of the Randolph Society were women; of the first fifteen members in 1930, only three were men -- Maurice Ellis, husband of Myrtle, Leonard Paine, husband of Ruth, and Primus Lamson. The other charter members were Jennie S. Allen, Nettie Crapo, May McClellan, Margery Flint, Irene Cheney, Emily Hutchinson, Cora Litchfield, Belle Morse, Mary Salisbury, and Emma Seymour.

Primus Lamson, co-owner with his brother of the Lamson's Hardware Store was well known throughout the area. Emily Hutchinson was the wife of a successful farmer in nearby Brookfield, and Mary Salisbury was the wife of a successful furniture manufacturer in Randolph.

Nettie Crapo and Irene Cheney served the Randolph field as practitioners, as did Ola Greene and Ora Martin, but in 1943, the Journal had no Randolph listing for a practitioner.

The first lecture given by the newly formed Randolph church was held September 15, 1932, and the speaker was John Randall Dunn, C.S.B.. Two years later, they gave a summer lecture, the speaker being Margaret M. Glenn, C.S.B.

The town of Bethel is just to the south of Randolph, and the following women were early workers in Bethel: Winifred Adams, Pauline and Louise Fisher, Hildegarde Challenger, Leslie and Marion Southworth, and Minnie Clifford.

Until 1946, the church had no permanent home but used local public buildings; since 1956, it has its own building on Main Street.

Barre, 1894

Mrs. Eddy made a second visit to Vermont in 1889 -- a working visit. She had become acquainted with a Vermont physician from Moretown, a rural community a few miles west of Barre. He took class from Mrs. Eddy in 1887, and shortly thereafter she legally adopted Dr.

Ebenezer Johnson Foster as her son. He took the name of Foster Eddy, and was for a few years an official at the Church headquarters, and infrequently joined Mrs. Eddy's household. [See Section One for further information about Foster Eddy.]

William Clark, a Barre resident and a colleague of Dr. Foster's during the Civil War, had a healing through Christian Science treatment of a life-threatening disease which had disabled him for more than twenty years. It was his healing that brought Dr. Foster into the study of Christian Science.

In the summer of 1889, Foster Eddy rented a house at #10 Park Street in Barre facing Currier Park and Mrs. Eddy came there with her secretary, Calvin Frye, and others. Mr. Clark was a frequent visitor, and in 1888, along with two others from the area, took Class Instruction from Mrs. Eddy. [See Section Four.] A few years later -- after Mrs. Eddy moved into Pleasant View -- he visited her there, and returned to Barre eager to begin a Society, and to be a listed practitioner. The earliest students met in Mr. Clark's home on Prospect Street. The first members were, as they appear in the January 25, 1949 "Historical Statement" report sent to The Mother Church:

> Mr. & Mrs. George A. Hill
> Mr. Irwin W. Bates
> Mrs. Cora Bates
> Mrs. Hattie Powers
> Mr. William Clark
> Mrs. Mary F. Celley
> Mr. & Mrs. S. Chamberlain
> Mr. Hiram Thayer

As the report states, "These ten students began holding services in rooms over Brown's Drug Store in October 1894." They were recognized as a branch the following year. The report states that they gave their first lecture in 1907, but that is incorrect. [See information below.] The report explains that in 1938, the members purchased an old residence, which was converted that year into a church hall, reading room, and three apartments. The first officers were:

President - William Clark, C.S.B.
Clerk - Mrs. Cora Bates
Treasurer - Mrs. Fannie B. Hill, C.S.
Directors - Mrs. Hattie Powers, C.S.;
    Sheran Chamberlain; and George A. Hill, C.S.
Auditor - Irving W. Bates

A hand-written note [Editor's note: a faded copy very hard to read!] accompanies the report and states:

So far as we are aware this was the first Christian Science Church organized and incorporated in Vermont. It may therefore not be out of place to give some of the events leading up to the organization. Miss Estelle Cheney, daughter of Mr. and Mrs. Lucius Cheney of East Barre, went to Boston as a student at Emerson School of Oratory. She heard of Christian Science and went through class with [illegible]. She came home and did some good healing work later going to Montreal.

Mrs. Ambrose B. Averill became interested in Christian Science. She loaned William Clark, who was an old soldier in very poor health who they did not expect to live long, Science and Health by Mrs. Eddy -- he was healed by reading the book. [Editor's note: We have another report stating that it was Mary Shipman Dillingham who loaned Wm. Clark the textbook.]

While there were Scientists holding meetings in their homes in Montpelier a few years before there was any formal activity in Barre, nevertheless, Barre became a formal Society in 1894 -- before both St. Johnsbury and Montpelier.

William Clark was the first listed practitioner in Barre. He was a pupil of Mrs. Eddy's in 1888, but was first listed in the Journal in November 1894. In 1898, a former Congregational minister, Rev. Sylvester C. Hayford, C.S.B. served both Barre and Montpelier. A year later Mr. Frank Walker and his wife Rose Walker were listed in Barre, and in 1907 Mrs. Walker was listed both as a practitioner and a teacher. She served in the Barre-Montpelier area until 1951. [See Section Four.]

In 1898, Reverend S.C. Hayford was listed in the Journal as the First Reader, and as a practitioner. While he lived in Montpelier, he spent one day a week in Barre as a practitioner. [See report on Burlington.]

In the August 9, 1890, Sentinel there were two notices from Barre under the heading: "Among the Churches." The first stated, "The attendance and interest in the services of First Church of Christ, Scientist, Barre, Vt., is increasing. In May 1900 a Reading Room was opened for the public in the room in which our services are held." The second was a personal statement from F.A. Walker (Frank A. Walker, C.S.):

> The wisdom of sending out the pamphlet "Christian Science History" in such large numbers has been partially shown to me by the way it has been received in some instances where I have been especially thanked for sending it. I have been glad to find it gives a more definite idea of the work of our Leader.

Barre

In the August 9, 1900 issue of the Sentinel is a testimony by a David Dawson of Barre. Mr. Dawson joined The Mother Church in 1899, his application having been endorsed by Mrs. Munroe and countersigned by Mrs. Walker. He remained a member of the Barre church until his passing in 1925. His testimony is reprinted in full at the close of this Barre Church report. Mrs. Celley, who lived in Calais some fourteen miles north of Barre and was a charter member, had her testimony published in the July 10, 1902 Sentinel. [See Section Four.] She joined The Mother Church in 1896 with William Clark as her countersigner, and remained a member in Barre until her passing in 1950.

On August 17, 1900, the Sentinel noted that Judge William G. Ewing of Chicago gave what was Barre's first lecture on Christian Science. He was introduced by the Honorable F.A. Howland, Vermont's Secretary of State. William McKenzie lectured for the Barre church on November 14, 1901.

In 1914, Mr. Walker was First Reader, and a Clayton Meaker was listed as the First Reader in 1915 as well as in 1918.

Mr. Dawson's testimony was printed in the August 9, 1900 Sentinel.

TOBACCO AND LIQUOR HABITS DESTROYED

It is nearly four years since I became interested in Christian Science. A friend gave me some Christian Science literature and asked me to read it. I did so, but as I had always possessed good health I paid very little attention to it. My friend

continued to give me literature from time to time. One day my eye caught something in the Journal that seemed to me to be sound common sense, and by reading a little more I learned that Christian Science was quite different from what I had thought it to be. My friend then loaned me "Science and Health with Key to the Scriptures." I set to work to find out all I could. I had not read very long before I pronounced it the most wonderful book I had ever seen. Well do I remember how I enjoyed reading that book! I could not have been more interested and delighted over a gold mine had I discovered one, and to-day after nearly four years of patient and persistent study, it is worth more to me than all the gold the world has ever seen.

Before I began the study of Christian Science my custom was to sit down every night after supper with my jug of beer, my pipe, and my newspaper, and read and smoke and drink until it was time to go to bed. I commenced to read Science and Health in my usual way, with my pipe and jug of beer, and would sit reading until morning. Often I went to bed just because I thought I had read enough for one night. After I had been reading Science and Health about a month my wife informed me that my beer was nearly gone and I had better see about getting another barrel. I told her that I thought I would not get any more beer. I wanted to get a copy of Science and Health of my own instead of the beer. She said I could please myself about it, but told me it was foolish of me to think I could get along without the beer when I had used it over thirty years, and had proved that I could not get along without it.

About a year previous to this I had made up my mind to stop drinking and did not drink anything for over six weeks. The result was that I lost flesh to such an alarming extent that I became frightened and commenced drinking again. I soon

regained my usual weight. My wife knew this and used it in support of her argument. I admitted the fact but told her my mind was made up to buy Science and Health and let the beer go, that I should now prove the truth of what I had been reading. I bought the book in place of the beer, and the result is that instead of losing flesh I am to-day thirty pounds heavier than I ever was before. My pipe was consigned to the stove about the same time, and now for over three years I have neither smoked nor drank, nor do I have the least desire to do so.

I love and cherish that book more than any other earthly possession. It has taught me to love and enjoy the beautiful. It has made me a happy man. I have put in use what little knowledge I have. I have treated many persons with good results. I have never had class instruction. My teacher has been Science and Health. I take the *Journal* and *Sentinel*, and how I do long for their coming.

Another case was that of a lady who wore glasses for years. In less than six months she could and can now see to set the finest work without glasses.

David Dawson, Barre, Vt

Christian Science

Rutland, 1894

Volume 4 of the Sentinel dated February 13, 1902, contained a brief notice about Rutland, Vt., under the heading "Among the Churches."

> First Church of Christ, Scientist of Rutland, Vt., was organized under the laws of the state, November 26, 1901, with twenty charter members. In December, 1898, we secured rooms for public services and the work has slowly but steadily progressed, until now we have an average attendance of about twenty. On the third of October [1901] a lecture was given by Judge Ewing, which was well attended, and cannot fail to bring forth much fruit. We all feel very grateful for the many blessings which have come to us through our understanding of Christian Science.
>
> Grace L. Bosworth, Clerk

A report sent to The Mother Church History Department suggests that Rutland's beginning interest in Christian Science started when a Mrs. Esther Abraham sent a copy of *Science and Health* to a William Wolff and his sister in 1894. The same report gives the names of twelve women who were charter members when the Society was formed.

Esther T. Abraham	Carrie Abraham
Frederika Abraham	Helen Ross
Grace Bosworth	Agnes Bosworth
Mildred Premo	Emily Premo
Lizzie Premo	Cynthia Bloomer
Evelyn Beals	Mary Townsend

Rutland

The September <u>Journal</u> for 1912 carried an article about the Rutland church under the heading "Progress of Christian Science." Excerpts, repeating original spelling and punctuation, follow:

> In the year 1896 [now thought to be 1894] two students of Christian Science came to Rutland, and for a time held services in their parlors. Only a very few persons attended, but after these students left the meetings were continued for two years in the homes of some of those who had become interested, public rooms first being rented in December 1898. After holding public services in a Society, First Church of Christ, Scientist, was organized in November, 1901, with twenty charter members, and for eleven years, as its varying needs demanded, the church occupied rooms in several different places.
>
> In April, 1911, arrangements were made by which a very desirable building lot centrally located was secured.... The building of the church was most harmonious, the entire amount required for the edifice having been paid in full, although there is still an encumbrance on the land.... The main audience-room...is capable of seating two hundred people. The location of the church is excellent, being in the residential section but very convenient to the business center of the city and easily accessible to all car lines.
>
> From a handful of worshipers, meeting here and there in rooms and small halls, the growth in the past thirteen years has been slow but steady, though many who were formerly members have moved elsewhere and are now working in other fields. The building of the church has therefore been a remarkable demonstration. The sense of love and unity which has prevailed, and without which Christian Science cannot progress, has made this possible. To see the beautiful church established by

the few faithful ones, is to know that it is indeed founded on the rock Christ Jesus, and is striving to fulfil his command to heal the sick, to bind up the broken-hearted, and to loose those bound in trespasses and sins.

When Mrs. Eddy established the By-law stating that practitioners must not have their offices in a church building or reading room space [1909], Stella Haddon Alexander, C.S.B. had to vacate the premises in downtown Rutland. But she was not the first "listed" practitioner there. Back in 1891, while the Journal was being published by the National Christian Scientists' Association, Mr. and Mrs. (Elmer and Lottie) Goding were listed in West Rutland. In 1898, the Godings were listed under West Randolph. Also listed in Rutland in 1898, was Charles S. Van Auker, with an office in the Ripley Block, and Helen B. Ross at #88 Church Street.

The Godings do not appear in the Journal for 1905, nor does Mr. Van Auker. Mrs. Alexander, in 1905, was one of three practitioners in Rutland, one of whom, Helen B. Ross became a teacher the following year (C.S.B.); the other was Mrs. Esther Abraham. [See Section Four.] A letter to the editor from Newman Weeks in the Rutland News for March 31, 1902, spoke approvingly of the fact that the indictment (the charge was fraud) of a Helen Wilmans Post for professing to cure by absent treatment in Christian Science had been quashed. The newspaper gave the letter the title of: "Righteous Judgment."

We do know that there were six children in the Sunday School as early as 1904. The following letter which was published in the July 16, 1904, issue of the Sentinel, first sent to Mrs. Eddy, was sent by Mrs. Eddy to the editor of the Sentinel along with this note:

"Received from the darling children of the Sunday School $20.00 -- M.B.G. Eddy."

Rutland, Vt., July 5, 1904

Beloved Leader: -- My heart yearns for words with which to express in love and gratitude to you as I send this gift from our little Sunday School of six children. The sum is small, but the largest gift to you has not carried with it more genuine and loyal love and gratitude. It is the desire of these little ones that you expend the enclosed sum upon some article to be used in the room set apart for you in the new church in Concord [New Hampshire], and may it ever remind you that the seed of your noble effort has taken root in Rutland. I am sure that it will gladden your faithful heart to know that since I wrote you last year, the work of Truth has steadily advanced here, much good fruit being in evidence to prove the healing power of Truth. And now, to you, dear Leader and friend, -- the one who has made all this possible for us, -- to you there go loving greetings to-day, from the little church in Rutland, Vt.

Obediently yours,
HELEN S. B. ROSS [C.S.B.]

David K. Smith, Professor of Economics Emeritus, Middlebury College, and his brother Larry grew up in the Rutland Sunday School where their parents (L.E. and Eleanor Smith) were very active for more than fifty years. Prof. Smith was one of the first members of the Middlebury Church; meanwhile his aunt, Mrs. Eunice Dizer, C.S., was one of the early members of the branch in Bellows Falls. Prof. Smith

recalls one long-time faithful member in Rutland, McRay Haskins, confessing, "I remember him mostly because he wore spats."

The elder Smiths founded a summer camp in Pittsford, Vermont (Sangamon for boys in 1922; their daughter, Jean Smith Davies, founded Betsey Cox for girls in 1953). Camp Sangamon advertised solely in The Christian Science Monitor. Campers were not limited to children of Christian Scientists, but a significant number of them attended Christian Science Sunday Schools. When the elder Smiths moved to Vergennes, they continued their membership in Rutland, making the long trip twice a week. Mrs. Smith, though not listed in the Journal, was an active practitioner. Her husband, a teacher and director of the Boys Club in Pittsford, served two terms in the Vermont Legislature.

Larry Smith, longtime director of Sangamon, recalled that a Mrs. Prouse, whose family owned Prouse's Restaurant in downtown Rutland, was a very active member. During the 1938 hurricane, when electricity was cut off throughout the Rutland region, the readers used candles and carried on.

In 1905, the church members met in the Dunn Building on Merchants Row; in 1910, they met at 87 West Street; and in 1915 were located at No. 8 Cottage Street.

Larry Smith remembers that the auditorium was filled with pairs of folding chairs. The Sunday School met upstairs in a small room also used as the Reading Room. The Sunday School pupils stayed on the left side of the church and went upstairs after the second hymn. When that space became crowded, his dad sectioned off

Rutland

a small portion of the foyer with glass doors. Most of the foyer was used as a Reading Room sales area during the week.

The June 28, 1913 Sentinel carried a testimony by Elsa Owen of Rutland. [See Section Four.] In 1914 Mrs. Abraham. C.S. and Mrs. Ross, C.S.B. were still listed in the Journal. [See Section Four.] In 1910 Miss Fannie C. Wilcox was the First Reader, in 1914 it was Mrs. Jennie B. Phillips, and in 1918 the First Reader was Miss Grace E. Bosworth.

A Mrs. White, who provided a recreation area for the city of Rutland, gave the Rutland church the funds to erect a new building on the main route between Rutland and Woodstock. They were able to sell their first building to the Greek Orthodox congregation, and were able to dedicate free of debt soon thereafter.

A well-known local musician, Mrs. Maynard Welsh, was the organist for more than fifty years. Interestingly, Barbara Duke, an accomplished pianist in Springfield, also served the branch there for some fifty years although she remained a member of the Baptist Church.

Christian Science

Burlington, 1896

Several of Vermont's branches got their start in kitchens and living rooms, where neighbors shared healing thoughts with neighbors. Not so Burlington; it began on shipboard on Lake Champlain in the summer of 1896. A Mrs. May Jones, C.S. (wife of a University of Vermont professor) and Mrs. Alma Porter Clark, C.S. were visiting together on the deck and reading Christian Science literature when two couples (Frank and Lottie Bowman and Homer and Clara Drury) began talking with them to learn about this new religion. Soon the two couples, Mrs. Jones, and a third couple, the Gilberts, began attending services held in Mrs. Clark's apartment at the local Hotel Van Ness. Both the Drurys and the Bowmans took class instruction, and Mrs. Eddy, from 1908 through 1910, employed the Bowmans at Chestnut Hill. [See Section Four.]

The seven were joined by the Armstrongs, Mrs. Ring, Mrs. Foster, and Reverend Hayford. [Most probably this is the same Rev. S.C. Hayford who had been active earlier in the Barre Church.] Both Mrs. Jones and Mrs. Foster advertised as Christian Science practitioners as soon as they could in the Christian Science periodicals. They were soon able to become a branch church with Mrs. Clark, Reverend Sylvester, and Mrs. Bowman joining them as public practitioners.

In the 1898 Journal, Mrs. Clark was listed as the First Reader in First Church, Burlington, and their Reading Room was open Mondays and Wednesdays from 2-4 P.M. At the same time, a group of Christian Scientists met in nearby Essex Junction, Sundays only, and were listed in the same volume of the Journal. The

Burlington

November 1899 Journal contained a long testimony by Sylvester C. Hayford of Burlington, Vt. We reprint some excerpts from that testimony here:

> It is now five years since I accepted Christian Science. I had been ill for many years, besides being at sea as to what to do for my spiritual salvation. Previously I had been in the ministry for over twenty-five years. I shall never forget how the Truth dawned upon me during my first treatment.... I knew from the spiritual uplifting I felt that I had come at last to the Truth. My beliefs, which had been considered serious, soon were overcome. Then came the more difficult task of overcoming sin, especially sin in thought. I have made perhaps some slow progress, but I know I am on the sure foundation.... More and more do I realize that every part of the work and organization of the great movement is ordained by God.... I have known enough of the unrest of merely **human** theories and **human** guidance. Having found the sweet assurance of acceptance with God and how to know Him, and having learned the way of Harmony, I can only say, let me press on with greater love and loyalty. Henceforth I cast away all repining and resolve to give myself unreservedly to Truth, and pray that all my strength may be given to build up God's order on earth, as revealed through His chosen agent, our Mother, Mary Baker Eddy.
>
> Sylvester C. Hayford, Burlington, Vt.

A clipping from the October 16, 1901 issue of the Burlington Free Press tells that "the members of the local Christian Science church and their friends entertained the Carl Behr String Quartette at the Van

Ness Parlors." The brief article explains that Mr. Behr, solo cellist of the festival orchestra of the Boston Symphony, is a Christian Scientist, and pronounces the recital as having been "delightful."

In 1899, on October 24, William McKenzie lectured for the Burlington Society; the following year, Irving C. Tomlinson, then First Reader in First Church, Concord, New Hampshire, was the lecturer. The third lecture was given by Judge Ewing on November 2, 1902, who had lectured four days before in St. Johnsbury, and two days before in Brattleboro. Vol. 5 of the Sentinel (p. 204) carried the following report reprinted from the Burlington Free Press:

> Judge William G. Ewing of Chicago spoke to a large audience in the Howard Opera House Sunday afternoon on "Christian Science: Physician and Redeemer."
>
> The Hon. Robert Roberts introduced the speaker in substance as follows:
>
> > In contemplation of the Infinite and the search after religious truth, the mind wanders far and wide. It has always been so. No repressive influence has ever been able to bind it or to circumscribe it. From time to time some prophet, true or false, is heard to cry, "Eureka! I have found it -- a new light for the soul; from the heights I have spied out a happy land of promise where many wanderers may find rest and peace." It is generally wise to give ear to the new voice. It may bring us glad tidings; but if not, it will only add one more to the many disappointments of the inquisitive spirit. Many of us cannot understand precisely what Christian Science is. A distinguished gentleman has come to tell us about it. I bespeak for him a fair hearing.

But when several members moved away and two factions developed, the church disbanded in 1908. Meetings were held in private homes for a few years in Burlington and Essex Junction, and then two remarkable healings of two local businessmen spurred the Scientists into re-forming. One of the businessmen was a prominent fur merchant (Charles M. Spear), and well known in Burlington. The other was Arthur C. Whitney who became a practitioner, the Committee on Publication for Vermont, then a teacher, and served as a lecturer for many years. Mr. Spear gave up his fur business and became a listed practitioner.

By 1913 this new organization with some twenty members was recognized by The Mother Church; in 1914, the society gave a lecture (Jacob S. Shield) and in 1920 was recognized as a branch. In 1914, Mr. Spear was the first reader; in 1915, that office was held by Mr. Whitney. And in 1914, only Charles Spear, C.S. was listed as a practitioner in Burlington. In 1915, a Mrs. Ada Foster, C.S. was listed in Burlington. [See Section Four.] Mrs. Foster had a poem and two articles printed in the Sentinel in 1903, 1909, and 1910. She also had three articles in the Journal in 1900, 1901, and 1902.

In 1918 the First Reader was Mrs. Clara E. Drury, the same Mrs. Drury who met with the other local Scientists on board ship on Lake Champlain twenty-two years previously -- in 1896.

No sooner had the Burlington/Essex Junction Christian Scientists settled their organizational differences than The Mother Church had an organizational upheaval that pitted the Trustees of the Publishing Society against the self-perpetuating Board of Directors of The Mother Church. Around the world, Societies and Branches wrestled with whether to

subscribe or advertise in the Publishing Society magazines. The dispute erupted outside the church administration into the Massachusetts court. On March 24, 1920, the members of First Church of Christ, Scientist, Burlington voted not to buy or distribute literature published by The Christian Science Publishing Society in Boston, with the exception of the writings of Mary Baker Eddy. They also voted to remove their card from the Journal.

The dispute was settled by the Supreme Court of Massachusetts, finding in favor of the Board of Directors and against the trustees of the Publishing Society. The Burlington branch, along with many others around the world, replaced their cards in the monthly Journal, and the little Burlington church prospered.

They bought a lot and built a church in 1927, opening it with a lecture on December 1, 1927, by Professor Hermann S. Herring. For a few years, the Reading Room was in the church, but in 1933, it was moved to the downtown business area.

The Journal for July 1900 contains a testimony with only the initials "I.M.N." datelined Burlington, and the Sentinel for December 6, 1930, contains a testimony by Mrs. Elsa Constans Holden of Burlington. [See Section Four.]

In 1944, three practitioners were active in Burlington: Mrs. Dora M. Clark, C.S.; Mrs. Maude C. Harrod, C.S.; and Mrs Jeannette Stewart Worden, C.S. [See Section Four.]

Newport, 1898

The present clerk, Ann C. Vining (niece of a founding member), kindly searched the old records, and provided the following report:

> The first known local interest in Christian Science occurred in the early fall of 1898, in what was then called "West Derby," the present east side of Newport City. Mrs. Ney Sleeper and her three children from New York City came to West Derby to visit a relative. While there her oldest child became very ill. Since Mrs. Sleeper was a Christian Scientist she relied upon prayer and her religion for healing. This was shocking and unheard of in West Derby, and Mrs. Sleeper was asked to leave the relative's home. However, this child was completely healed and the customary quarantine was unnecessary. Several persons in West Derby approached Mrs. Sleeper either to acquaint her with their interest in Christian Science or to ask questions about it.
>
> The authorized testimony of this healing was published in the "Christian Science Journal." [We have been unable to locate this account.] As far as is known, this was the first demonstration in the Town of Derby of a malady healed through Christian Science. Mrs. Ney Sleeper is Elizabeth G. Sleeper of West Derby, Vt., who had a testimony in the Sentinel (September 6, 1900) telling of the healing of cramps by a fellow Scientist in the area, and of her serving as the practitioner to heal the same man of "a terrible shock." [This testimony can be found in Section Four.] Mrs. Sleeper's granddaughter, Phyllis Hammond, is a member today of the Newport Society.
>
> In the summer of 1913, there is a record of four Sunday services held with a collection of $20.46

taken by T. E. Woodruff. In 1915, Kathleen W. Robinson was healed through Christian Science after her father contacted a practitioner in Boston. Matthew J. Robinson of West Derby was interested in Christian Science, and encouraged his family and others in its study and use. Several of these friends joined in attending Sunday services in the homes of Mr. and Mrs. Clarence Bugbee, Mr. and Mrs. William True, and Colonel and Mrs. Curtis Emery. It was in 1923 that they became a branch of The First Church of Christ, Scientist, Boston, Massachusetts.

The records show that the first regular service was held on August 10, 1919, and from that date 145 services were held in homes, and eleven more services were held in the Chapel. On March 22, 1922, at a business meeting held at the home of Mr. and Mrs. Carl White, the decision was made to take a five-year lease on the Universalist Chapel on East Main Street in Newport -- with an option to purchase for $1,500.

On September 19, 1922, a month later, the records show that a Mrs. Herman of Boston was invited to visit Newport "with the view of coming later as a practitioner." Three weeks later (October 3), with Mrs. Herman and seven other Scientists being present, it was reported that The Mother Church could not help pay the expenses for a lecture until the group became an organized Society.

A little more than a year later there were sufficient members, and on December 16, 1923, it was voted unanimously to organize as the Christian Science Society of Newport. Three weeks later (January 6, 1924), the following twelve persons signed the application for society status:

Newport

Alice House	Geneva T. Paterson
Harriet J. Emery	Nellie E. White
Doris E. Emery	Hazel Ball Fee
Marie C. Blanchard	Emma Buckland
Nellie G. Brooks	Minnie Smith
Carl A. White	Kathleen Robinson

On December 1, 1924, a deed was recorded for the purchase of the Universalist Chapel on East Main Street. With a gift of $1,045.80 from the Trustees Under the Will of Mary Baker Eddy, the Newport Society cancelled its debt for the church edifice. On November 30, 1925, the Society became an authorized branch.

Lyndonville, some thirty-five miles south of Newport began holding services before 1910, even though Lyndonville is less than ten miles north of St. Johnsbury.

The Journal for September 1912 carried a fairly long testimony by Mrs. C.S. Emery [Harriet] telling how three years earlier she had turned successfully to Christian Science for help in healing mental depression. [See Section Four.] If our records are correct, Mrs. Emery and her daughter Doris joined The Mother Church in 1913, their applications having been endorsed and countersigned by two Vermonters: Katherine Puffer of St. Johnsbury, and Emma Shipman, originally from Danville. Mrs. Emery had one article and two poems published in the Sentinel in 1917, 1920, and 1921.

We know, too, that when Mrs. Eddy was in Barton in 1884, she made a day trip to Newport. It's possible she just went for the scenery, and that there

Christian Science

were no students of Christian Science in the area known to her.

As far as we know, Newport held Sunday services from 1923 through 1953, then it had no Journal listing for 1954 or 1955. But in 1956, it was once again holding public services.

Brattleboro, 1898

In 1886, the Journal published by the Christian Scientists' Association had 83 practitioners and teachers advertising through "cards"; i.e., the healer placed an advertisement in the Journal in the form of a type of "calling card." One of those listed in 1886 and again in the 1887 volume was a Mrs. Mary E. Morse, C.S., of No. 50 Organ Street, whose advertisement read: "Patients visited at their home, if desired." Mrs. Morse advertised in February 1885 from Cambridgeport, Massachusetts. Then, from November 1885 through May 1887, she gave Brattleboro as her address. [See Section Four.]

Lucy Gilman, a member of The Mother Church, moved to Brattleboro in 1898, and began holding

Brattleboro

Sunday readings of the Bible Lesson-Sermon in her home. Others began joining in, and they soon outgrew the home and rented public space. By 1902, they held their first public lecture on Christian Science, and in 1904, were recognized as First Church of Christ, Scientist. Mrs. Gilman, C.S. had her listing in the Journal beginning in 1900. Along with Lucy Gilman, Jennie Chandler, Nellie and Joseph Brasor, and Gertrude Chandler retained their membership in Brattleboro from 1904 for the rest of their lives.

The Sentinel for November 27, 1902 (p.203), reprinted the following from the Vermont Phoenix, a local Brattleboro newspaper:

> The followers of the Christian Science religion in Brattleboro are entitled to entertain feeling of pride at the success of their efforts to bring before the Brattleboro public the essential elements of their doctrine. The lecture by Judge William G. Ewing of Chicago in the Auditorium last evening [October 30], under the auspices of the Christian Science Society of Brattleboro, drew an audience that packed the floor and the first balcony.

The Sentinel of August 15, 1903, contained testimony by a Mrs. Ida Miller of Brattleboro. We reprint it here:

> It is with thankfulness for this great truth, as set forth by Mrs. Eddy in Science and Health, that I write of my healing.
>
> Early in April, 1902, while walking on the street, I was suddenly taken with a severe pain in my left side. I walked home with difficulty, the pain clinging to me night and day.

I did not call a doctor at once, thinking it would pass away, as I called myself a well woman.

As time passed and I seemed no better, I of course saw a doctor, and he said I must have an operation, as I had a growth. I made up my mind then and there that no operation should be performed on me.

One day as I was sitting in my misery a lady came in who had read Science and Health, and understood something of the healing. She encouraged my trying Christian Science, and I was ready to do anything rather than undergo an operation, and told her so.

The lady then said, "I will help you as best I know; I am not a practitioner, but if you will read Science and Health, I will give you good thoughts, as I know them; and remember, if you falter once I give you up immediately." She has been faithful, and when I tell you that I am a well woman to-day you may know I have not faltered or turned back once.

I say this to encourage all who are in physical trouble to go at once to this scientific method of healing, and by clinging to it, regardless of the seeming, you certainly will conquer as so many others have.

Mrs. Ida Miller, Brattleboro, Vt.

The Journal for April 1916 carried a pair of testimonies from Mr. E. Frederick and Mrs. Marjorie A. Coxson. [See Section Four.]

In 1910, a Mrs. Fanny G. Miles was the First Reader. In 1914, Mrs. Gilman, C.S. was listed in Brattleboro as a practitioner, as was a Mrs. Etta Chamberlain, C.S. A Mrs. Elizabeth Nathan, C.S. was listed in Putney just a few miles north of Brattleboro. [See Section Four.] That year, John L. Lawton was the First Reader. In 1918 the first reader was Mrs. Rose Osborn.

At a regular business meeting in 1919, the twenty-seven members present discussed whether or not to buy a prominent lot available from Mrs. Estey (of the Estey Organ Co. family) for $6,500. Fourteen voted in favor of this gigantic step. Mrs. Estey kindly took a low-cost mortgage, and since the lot included a house, the members were able to sell it. Part of their funds were tied up in World War I Liberty Bonds, which were used over the years to complete the purchase.

On November 25, 1920, Thanksgiving Day, a cornerstone was laid that included the *Bible*, *Science and Health*, and *The Mother Church Manual*. All available charter members were in attendance. Noting that the winter was mild, the building was completed the following summer; and the first Sunday service was held in July. On October 18, 1930, all indebtedness was canceled, allowing for dedication.

Bennington, 1900

To quote from the official history:

In the year 1900 there were three earnest seekers of the truths of Christian Science in Bennington. They were Mrs. Lucy E. Rockwood, Mrs. Annie S. Cooper, and Mrs. Jennie D. Carrier. These ladies met often on Sunday afternoons to read and ponder the lesson-sermons of the quarterly. Friends were invited, and so attendance grew.

Regular Sunday gatherings began to be held, early in 1902, at the home of Mrs. Rockwood.

In 1906, for the sake of a more central location, the readings were transferred to the home of Mr. and Mrs. Charles Cooper.

On December 9, 1906, the services were moved to a room on the corner of Park and Scott Streets. This room was equipped and given for the use of services by Mr. Cooper. Wednesday evening meetings were held. A Sunday school of six pupils and two teachers was established. Here the Christian Science Society of Bennington, Vermont, was organized, with public services advertised in the Christian Science Journal of July 1909.

A sheet from the official record book contains the heading, "Agreement for Members First Meeting." The information follows:

"The undersigned, being all of the signers of the Articles of Association of Christian Science Society of Bennington, Vermont, Inc., hereby agree that we will voluntarily assemble for the purpose of holding the first meeting for the organizing of said corporation, said meeting to be held in the Society's Reading Room in

Bennington on Monday afternoon, May 20th, 1918, at three o'clock P.M., and we further hereby consent that if we are not present, the same preceedings may be had at such meeting as if we were personally present and had received any other and further notice that the statutes might require."

The first eleven members, in the order given in the record book were:

    Mrs. W.J. Hicks *   Mrs. Anna S. Carpenter *
    Mrs. Anne Cooper *   Mrs. Jennie D. Carrier
    Mrs. Carrie Hynick   Mr. Conrad Hynick
    Mrs. L.C. Rockwood   Miss S.A. Upham
    Mrs. Elizabeth H. Moore Miss Fanny S. Carrier
        Miss Ruth D. Carrier

The first three (*), were the only ones to meet that afternoon to adopt the by-laws. On the 1st day of May, 1918, the same eleven members were the official "subscribers" to the Vermont Secretary of State for official recognition as the Christian Science Society of Bennington, Vt, Inc. Other members who had joined the Society by 1918 were: Henry E. Burgess, Charles Patterson, Miss Mary L. Heutshins, Mrs. Jane Graves Mousarrat, Mrs. Elizabeth H. Morse, Mrs. Mary F. Cummins, Mrs. Marilla A. Hicks, Emerson M. Torrey, Mrs. Florence A. Kipp, and Mrs. Margaret M. Estes.

The Bennington Society gave its first lecture on June 9, 1916; the speaker was Virgil O. Strickler of New York City.

A 1937 issue of <u>Bennington Banner</u> reported the dedication of the building for the First Church of Christ, Scientist, Bennington, and listed, as "first members" Mr. & Mrs. John F. Quinby, Mr. & Mrs. Melvin W.

Stewart, a Miss M.W. Thorn, Samuel Smith and Mrs. Rockwood, Mrs. Cooper, Mrs. Carrier, and the Misses Fanny and Jennie Carrier. This list is slightly different from the one apparently taken directly from an old Church record book.

When the Society moved to First Church status in 1928, one of the two co-signers of the official papers was one of the first members, Fanny S. Carrier. Then, in 1936, the daughter of first member Annie Semple Cooper gave the Church's building fund $40,000. At the dedication services, the First Reader concluded a short history stating, "...and today we humbly, gratefully dedicate this beautiful church building to the worship of God in Spirit and in Truth."

The Church records also tell that Mrs. Rockwood had been a member of The Mother Church since 1903, and continued her membership in Bennington until her passing in 1933. Mrs. Cooper, Mrs. Carrier, and Miss Fanny S. Carrier had joined The Mother Church in 1906.

In 1910, a Mrs. Harriet Hovey Rogers was the First Reader. The first practitioner, Mrs. Georgianna S. Quinby, C.S., if we are correct, was listed in the Journal in 1914. That same year, Mrs. Alma S. Carpenter was the First Reader. Miss Fannie Carrier was the First Reader in 1918.

In 1943, there were two practitioners serving the church, one who lived in North Bennington -- Miss Evelyn Paine, C.S. -- and one in town -- Mrs. Minnie L. Peckham, C.S. The early records show that Miss Paine joined Bennington's Church on January 6, 1929, and The Mother Church in 1930. Mrs. Peckham joined The Mother Church in 1920, and the Bennington Church on

June 12, 1929; she was still active as a practitioner in Bennington in 1943. [See Section Four.]

St. Albans, 1904 - 1913

We have not been able to locate an "official" history of the St. Albans branch, yet in 1898, Mrs. Mary Waite Warren, C.S. was listed in the Journal with an office in the St. Albans Opera House. But by October 1904, Mrs. Warren and her family (four daughters and a son) had moved to Montpelier where Mrs. Warren and her oldest daughter Mary Alethea were charter members of that Society.

In 1902, Miss Margaret J. Axtell, C.S. moved to East Berkshire from Boston, and was listed in the September 1904 Journal at 118 Main Street in St. Albans. East Berkshire is a small town some twenty-five miles west of St. Albans on the Missisquoi River. Miss Axtell was a practitioner in Boston from November 1895 to October 1902. Mrs. Anna B. Hale, C.S. lived at 21 Messenger Street in the city, joined The Mother Church in 1904, and was a listed practitioner there until she moved to California in 1916. And Miss Jane E. Rankin, C.S. was First Reader for the St. Albans Society in 1904, and began her practitioner listing in March 1906. She

remained in St. Albans until her passing in 1929. [See Section Four.]

The St. Albans Society met at #4 Kingman Street beginning in September 1904, but were forced to disband in May 1907. The Mother Church History Department's records show that the Society began holding public meetings again in April 1909. Their records show the Society closing in September 1913. Miss Rankin had an office in the Society's rooms which she was in daily from 10 A.M. to 1 P.M., and home calling hours were 2-5 P.M. The St. Albans Society met on Sunday at 11 A.M., Wednesdays at 7.30 P.M., and kept the Reading Room open daily.

The Journal shows St. Albans beginning Sunday services in 1904, and ending them in 1914. They had their first lecture on May 21, 1905; the speaker was Judge Septimus J. Hanna. The 1910 Journal listed Anna B. Hale as the First Reader.

The following testimony of Mrs. Hale's appeared in the August 20, 1904 issue of the Sentinel:

> A year ago last March, Christian Science came to me and I supposed that in common with that of other churches this was a beautiful religion, but the healing by the prayer of understanding I could not then grasp or believe. One day I was taken ill, and after much distress said to my husband, "Isn't it too bad after all I've gone through and suffered by the physicians' advice, and the number that I've had (twenty-one in all), I still am not well, and not one day ahead can I ever feel safe to make a plan, my health is so uncertain. I shall have no more operations, but will do the best I can and try to endure the suffering with patience when it comes, but I believe I'll try Christian Science first. It cannot

do me any harm if it's of God, and then I shall feel that I have done all in my power to be well and of some use in the world."

The next day I said to the Christian Science practitioner, "If you think you can help me, I wish you'd try." She did and I was cured immediately. I have never had a return of the trouble, and have been able to walk miles. It was an ovarian trouble, and the physician's advice was that if one operation failed to cure, there must be a second; but I never had the second operation. It had taken me several years to get over the nervous shock of the first one, and the opinion was that I would in time be 'comparatively well' only.

Last fall another old trouble which used to keep me down appeared in a severe attack. It was a serious rectal ailment of long standing. Eight years ago I had ten tumors removed, a few at a time. My husband finally said nothing more should be done. The last operation kept me in bed a month, suffering so intensely that it took months to recover strength.

Christian Science again came to my rescue with an immediate cure. The dear practitioner came on the noon train, and left me free from pain at six, to return home. It took a little time for the swelling to subside so I could stand or sit or even lie on my back, but in three days I was busy doing a little housework, and in ten days, besides doing housework, I walked two miles, not simply to see what could be done, but I felt like walking, and knew that street cars were available in case of need. There has been no return of that trouble nor of constipation.

I have studied my Bible as never before, in the new light which Science and Health has shed upon it, and have had many demonstrations for myself and others, and also on a sick animal, to prove that

Christian Science

God's promises are safe and sure as in the time of Jesus. I am very thankful and grateful to those two kind practitioners who helped me to this new and beautiful understanding, and to Mrs. Eddy, through whom it has become possible, by her untiring devotion and loyalty. God indeed has been very good to me.

A.B.H., St. Albans, Vt.

Bellows Falls, 1906 - 1965

The first meetings were held in private homes, and at least one of those locations was a large working farm south of the town alongside the Connecticut River. The first to meet at the home of Mr. and Mrs. Lord, were Mrs. Thompson, Mrs. Parker, Mrs. Gast, Mrs. Barnard, and Mrs. Black. This information has come from a report filed with The Mother Church on January 5, 1948 by Julia Kusterer, clerk. To quote directly:

These meetings continued for about three years [until] Mr. and Mrs. [Lord] returned to New York...

In 1926 Mrs. Eunice Dizer came here from Fitchburg, a tea was given by Mrs. George Ryder to those in town who were interested in Christian Science. At Mrs. Dizer's suggestion sixteen people

met on December 6, 1926 in her home, 24 School Street.

Mrs. Black was First Reader and Mrs. Haines Second Reader, both of whom were listed practitioners beginning in 1927.

On January 10, 1927 some twelve Scientists who lived in the area agreed to apply to The Mother Church for recognition as a branch. The following ten women and two men were the charter members.

Miss Frances Babbitt	Mrs. Louise Barnard
Mrs. Jennie S. Black	Mrs. Eunice Dizer
Mrs. Katherina Haines	Mrs. Mary Homer
Mrs. Ruth Jewett	Mr. D.H. Switzer
Mrs. Emma Switzer	Mrs. Jennie Thayer
Mr. Erwin Whitcomb	Mrs. Marie Winnewisser

The clerk closes the report explaining, "Though our growth seems slow, if we consider that of our 18 members only four of the original group remain, we can note some progress." Mrs. Switzer's testimony of a healing of the morphine habit is in Section Four, and although the healing took place in 1912, her testimony appeared in the May 13, 1916 Sentinel.

On August 23, 1953, the members were able to hold dedication services for the building which they had purchased in 1951 and, as the Bellows Falls Times stated, "completely transformed into a church with a free public reading room in the same building."

When Mrs. Eunice H. Dizer became a practitioner in 1934, the Society became First Church. Mrs. Dizer, Aunt Eunice to the Smith children who were early members in Rutland and Middlebury, joined The Mother Church in 1916 and taught school for several

years; one year at Kimball Union Academy located not far from Bellows Falls across the Connecticut River in New Hampshire, and for several years in the Greater Boston area. She took class instruction in 1927 and became a full-time practitioner in 1934, listed in Bellows Falls until 1943, and after that in New Jersey.

She was the Committee on Publication for Vermont from about 1930 until 1943. Mrs. Dizer addressed several Associations and had more than a dozen metaphysical articles published in the Monitor, Sentinel, and Journal.

Both Mrs. Dizer's son John, and her nephew Larry, recall how she used trains, wagons, and even sleds to get around to the various church groups in relation to her Committee on Publication Work. She provided many commemorative services for fellow Scientists who had passed away. Larry tells a wonderful story about Aunt Eunice getting her driver's license.

"She got her first Vermont drivers license in 1918 when all you had to do was have three people certify that they knew you had driven 100 miles on Vermont roads. In 1923, road tests were put in, but all those with licenses were 'grandfathered.' She did take a written test in 1943 when she moved to New Jersey."

When Mrs. Haines was no longer active as a practitioner, the Bellows Falls Church, with no practitioner and fewer than sixteen members, went back to Society status.

A history of the town of Rockingham published in 1958 contains a history of Christian Science in Bellows Falls written by Mr. Frances Lovell. He noted

that the Bellows Falls branch was one of some 3,100 branches worldwide. Some excerpts from the original article:

> The first public interest in Christian Science became manifest in Bellows Falls in 1906 when services were held in a private home for about three years. A church was advocated again in 1912, but not until December 6, 1926, when sixteen people met for [Sunday] services, was regular worship held in various homes....
>
> Thereafter services were held regularly, first in the Odd Fellows' Hall, later in the Woman's Club, and then at a private home...until July 1951 [when] the Society occupied the premises at #3 School Street, continuing Sunday morning services at 10.45 A.M., with Sunday School at the same hour, and its Reading Room open to members and the general public on Saturday afternoons from two to four.
>
> In April 1950 the Society voted to hold Wednesday Evening Services as well and [to] open the Reading Room on Wednesday afternoons as well as Saturday. In July 1951 the Society purchased the Clark Bowen residence at #39 School Street and moved into its new quarters August 1. Work was begun at once to transform this residence into a church which was finished at the end of November 1952. The removal of two walls on the first floor created a fair-sized auditorium, seating about fifty people. The Reading Room adjoins the auditorium and opens into the business office. The two Sunday school rooms are on the upper floor. A new Hammond organ provides music....
>
> The Reading Room is open to members and the general public for rest and study and the Bible, the Christian Science textbook, <u>Science and Health with Key to the Scriptures</u> by Mary Baker Eddy and

other books and periodicals on Christian Science may be read, borrowed, or purchased. The public is always welcome to all services.

In 1965 Bellows Falls Society disbanded and most of the remaining members went either to Brattleboro to the south, Springfield to the north, or east to Keene in New Hampshire.

Lyndonville, 1907 - 1975

In 1953, Miss Helen Coolidge of Lyndon, Vermont, wrote a history of the Christian Science Society. She started with a preamble: "The forming of a Christian Science Organization is a deeply significant event, significant because the organization becomes a part of a great revolution, the greatest of all modern times: the changing of human thought from a material to a spiritual basis."

She continued by explaining that the Society was initially formed on January 27, 1907 with eleven charter members.

> Interest was first awakened...in Lyndonville by the healing of Mrs. E.G. Parker in 1906. Mrs. Parker was told her case, consumption, was hopeless but hearing that in Littleton, New Hampshire, there

Lyndonville

was a Christian Science practitioner she called for help and was quickly and permanently healed...

After that healing, informal services, beginning in November 1906, were held in Albert Goss' apartment, upstairs in a house on Main Street near the creamery...

There were Sunday services only, in the beginning, later Wednesday evening meetings were held, a Reading room opened and a Sunday school organized...

The first lecture was given in 1910 by Mr. F.H. Leonard...

The organization has never been burdened with debt but has consistently given of its store both to churches and to individuals, when it seemed best, and to funds such as the Publishing House Fund, The Mother Church Extension Fund, War Relief, Flood Relief, and CARE.

On the other hand, they have been the recipient of a great deal of generosity. Mrs Carrie Jeffers, at one time gave $500. Mrs. Jennie Folsom bequeathed $3,000, with an additional $200 for each two years, following her passing on. Mr. Charles Darling returned the rent check of $10 a month, for many years and in other ways was a generous benefactor. From a town church fund, the Society also received a yearly donation.

She concluded the formal portion of the report with the following declaration: "Throughout the years, the workers have been faithfully plowing up the ground, sowing the seed and doing work that under the government of Principle connects with all spiritual work tending toward universal enlightenment."

Christian Science

The charter members were, in the order given in the report:

E.G. Parker	Irene E. Parker
Jennie D. Folsom	Emma B. Wells
Edna M. Hill	Cora W. Frasier
Emma M. Ide	Albert A. Goss
Mrs. A.A. Goss	M.M. Keough
F.E. Simpson	

Mr. and Mrs. Parker were the first two readers, and it seems that three who were not charter members, but who served "steadfast in the work of the Cause," deserved special mention. They were: Irene E. Stimson, Maud H. Watson, and Marian Sutton. Cora Frasier was the First Reader in 1910. Irene Stimson was the First Reader in 1915, and Dora M. Clark was the First Reader in 1918. The Society gave a lecture on February 18, 1916. The speaker was Frank Bell. This was somewhat rare, as most of the Vermont branches did not schedule winter lectures.

In May 1955, the present location of the church -- 25 Center Street -- was a building site; four months later the church was completed, and the first service there was a Wednesday evening testimony meeting. The church, free of debt, was dedicated on June 10, 1956. The plan for the church building was a copy of the Christian Science Church in Spencerport, New York.

A newspaper report described the building as "...a simple frame structure, painted white, suitable to be [in] a New England village. In the interior, the...Readers' desks are made of Philippine mahogany, with hangings of old gold and with a very delicate green tint on the walls."

Springfield/Chester, 1908

The Christian Science Society that today is located in Chester is the Society of Springfield, one town removed. The Springfield/Chester church started in Mrs. Lester Kane's home in Springfield when she and Mrs. Alice Wray read the Lesson-Sermon together. In 1932, Marie Reiners, then clerk, wrote, at the request of The Mother Church Archivist, a history (1908-1932), from which excerpts have been taken. Mrs. Reiners began by quoting a former clerk's one-sentence report.

> On the 5th day of May 1912, eleven persons met and voted to organize Christian Science Society of Springfield, Vermont." Nellie Murphy, Clerk

The organization of Christian Science had its beginning in the village of Springfield, Vermont, in the spring of 1908, when two ladies, Mrs. Lester E. Kane and Mrs. Alice Wray, met each Monday afternoon at the home of the former, to read the Lesson Sermon. In June 1908 they were joined by Mrs. Susie H. Morse and a little later by Mrs. Eliela Lovell. These meetings continued at the home of Mrs. Kane until February 1909, when Mrs. Kane left town and the same readings were continued at the home of Mrs. Morse. Shortly after this, Mrs. Wray left town also. In 1911, the time of the meetings was changed to Sunday morning. Three of those attending became members of The Mother Church, and thereafter the order of service followed that of The Mother Church.

Mr. Clarence E. Morse, Miss F. Ruth Morse, Mrs. Caroline Lovell, and Mrs. Raymond Lovell joined the congregation at this time. There has never been a break in the services from that time on, even though at times there were just two in the

Christian Science

congregation - and only four members in town. There were a number of early healings through the reading of the textbook - which brought much encouragement and inspiration.

In May, 1912, Christian Science Society of Springfield, Vermont, was organized, by-laws were adopted, and a card was placed in the Christian Science Journal. Names of the original members follow:

Mrs. Eliela Lovell (now in Watertown, Mass.)

Mrs. Helen J. Wood (left to join services in her own town and later passed on)

Mrs. Susie H. Morse (an active member)

Mr. Clarence E. Morse (an active member)

Mrs. Caroline Lovell (an active member)

Mr. Raymond Lovell (no longer a member)

Miss Lillian Kimball (left and has since passed on)

Mrs. Rosa J. Cross (withdrew)

Mr. James B. Mason (left town)

Mr. John A. Frazier (passed on)

Meetings were held at the home of Mr. and Mrs. Morse until January, 1913, when the place of meeting was changed to a public hall. Services were continued in various public halls for some years. In 1915, the first assistant to the State Committee on Publication was appointed, the first Distribution Committee was formed and authorized Christian Science literature was placed in the Springfield Public Library. In 1916, Mrs. Susie H. Morse became a registered practitioner and is still practicing here. In 1917, the first public lecture was given by Mr. William R. Rathvon. In 1918 Mrs. Helen J. Wood was the First Reader. The Sunday school was started in November, 1919, in a room adjoining the hall where services were being held. For a part of the year 1921, Wednesday evening testimonial meetings were held

twice a month, since the hall was available only on alternate Wednesday evenings, but these meetings were discontinued because of small attendance. A Reading Room was opened in April, 1926, in a room rented for that purpose.

In April, 1928, a big forward step was made possible. A letter was received from Mr. Norwood, Clerk of The Mother Church, stating that someone interested in this Society, but who wished his name withheld, wished to contribute towards a permanent home for the Society. This very loving offer was accepted and a desirable property at 90 Main Street was acquired. The society was incorporated under State laws, and the by-laws were adjusted to meet State requirements.

This permanent home has proved a most satisfactory one and each member of the society rejoices in this gift of divine Love. The Wednesday evening services were begun once more and have proved very helpful. The service room, Reading Rooms, and Sunday school rooms occupy the first floor ... The village of Springfield is one where machine shops supply the main industry and the population shifts, according to busy and dull seasons. For this reason, the members, both of the Church membership and of the congregation, have fluctuated - but the work of those early workers has remained established and has borne fruit. We, the members of Christian Science Society of Springfield, Vermont, rejoice in the presence of an established Christian Science organization in our midst - and wish to do our part in carrying on this great work.

Between 1932 and 1967, the house was converted to accommodate four apartments on the upper two floors, and the church rooms including a Reading Room were on the first floor. Marie Page (formerly Marie Reinert), in a report to The Mother Church, explained,

Christian Science

"We are happy to report that we are free from indebtedness. However, we are very low in membership at the present time; we seem to be just a handful of women! Many former members have moved away and we have no one to replace them."

The next report to The Mother Church by Judith W. Zeiser was in April 1980. She told of the previous lean years: "By 1967, the Society was struggling, they used Readers from other churches, no lectures had been given in ten years. The members were not strong in their reliance on Christian Science for healing. The contents of the church rooms were on loan."

Then the report of the fat years: "We have fifteen dedicated members of which one is a Christian Science Journal listed practitioner. We are able to rotate readers, conduct Sunday School with two classes and have a children's room. Our Reading Room is open on Saturdays for two hours. We have, at least, one Christian Science Lecture a year."

But by the winter of 1983, several members of the Society had moved out of town, and the non-church-related task of running an apartment house on top of church quarters was becoming prohibitive. The building was sold, and over the winter the Sunday services were held in a private residence until the First Universalist Parish in Chester agreed to rent their beautiful old stone church to the Society, allowing the Scientists to hold their Sunday services and Sunday School at 11 A.M., after the Unitarian Universalists had completed their meeting at 10 A.M.

Wilmington, Barnard, Northfield, Morrisville

Wilmington, 1910-1920

Barnard, 1911-1915

Northfield, 1918-1951

Morrisville, 1919-1942

> *In 1910, there were ten branches throughout Vermont -- five societies and five churches. The following year there were eleven. Unfortunately, the branches in Wilmington, Barnard, Northfield, and Morrisville closed before The Mother Church History Department began collecting early histories. We have been able to pick up some scattered information about the activities in these four areas.*

Wilmington: The <u>Sentinel</u> of October 4, 1900, contains a testimony from a D. Macdonald who was then teaching school in Readsboro, just a few miles southwest of Wilmington. The testifier was healed of nervous prostration. [See Section Four.] On January 14, 1913, in the <u>Sentinel</u> is a testimony by "Mrs. Gilbert P. Morris, Wilmington, Vt.," telling of a healing back in 1907. We reprint it here:

> Christian Science has done so much for me that I wish to tell of it, hoping thereby to encourage others who are in sickness and sorrow to study Science and Health and to be made free. Until I was

Christian Science

healed through the truth, in January 1907, I had never known what it was to be free from pain, and for many years I had seldom been without pain, and for many years I had seldom been without medicine. I was operated on for appendicitis, an abnormal growth, and other troubles, and exhausted the skill of fifteen kind physicians. I continued to grow worse, and felt that I had not long to stay in this world. This is where Christian Science found me, and it has brought me out of darkness and gloom, out of sickness and sorrow, into God's marvelous light. I have proven that to know God is eternal Life, and I am deeply grateful for the better understanding of God which I have gained through the study of this great truth.

I never had better health than at present, and I would like to add that through the study of Science and Health I have been enabled to lay aside glasses, after having used them for twenty years for defective vision, with near-sightedness. This is a proof to me that Christian Science is the truth which Jesus said would make us free. The physical healing which I have received has been great, but the spiritual uplifting is even greater, and I can truly say that the five years which I have spent in Christian Science are the happiest years of my life, and I should not care to live without the knowledge of this truth. I feel grateful to everyone who has in any way helped me in my journey from sense to Soul, and I am also grateful that there was one pure enough to voice this truth to a hungering world.

Mrs. Gilbert P. Morris, Wilmington, Vt.

Wilmington, Barnard, Northfield, Morrisville

The 1913 volume of the Sentinel tells that the Society in Wilmington was giving a lecture in Memorial Hall on February 21, 1913, at 8 P.M.

The Mother Church History Department provided information about three who were active in Wilmington while it was a branch of The Mother Church. William N. Bassett was the first First Reader in Wilmington beginning in August, 1910, when the Society has its first listing in the Journal. Lizzie E. Morris (perhaps that is the Mrs. Gilbert Morris whose testimony is in Section Four) was listed as First Reader beginning in May, 1912. And Mrs. Nellie M. Buckley began her term as First Reader in June 1918.

Mr. Bassett became a member of The Mother Church in 1900, and was a member of the Wilmington Society until his passing in 1920.

Lizzie Morris, who lived on Pleasant Street in Wilmington was a Baptist until she joined The Mother Church in 1911. Her application to join was endorsed by a Mrs. Gertrude E.M. Babcock, C.S., and countersigned by Mrs. Julia E. Prescott, C.S.D. Apparently Mrs. Babcock remained a member of the Wilmington Society until its closing.

Mrs. Buckley also joined The Mother Church in 1911, leaving the Methodist Episcopal faith to do so. Her application was endorsed by Mr. Bassett and countersigned by Irving C. Tomlinson, C.S.B. She, too, appears to have remained a member of the Wilmington Society until it closed.

Barnard: We have received no information about the Barnard Society. We do know, though that a Miss

Christian Science

Earlie Sacred Chase was the first First Reader in Barnard. The Journal for 1911 also listed Miss Earlie Chase, C.S., and Miss Lillie Rivers Chase, C.S., as practitioners in Barnard. [See Section Four.]

Northfield: First listing for public meetings was in the March 1918 Journal The First Reader was Mrs. Elizabeth B. Huntley; the Second Reader was Mrs. Lena M. Kerr. In December 1916, Mrs. Nellie L. Reed wrote to The Mother Church about the Society's "slow but steady" progress. First they met in private homes, then in 1915 they hired a public room first at 8 Central Street, then at 18 South Main Street.

Morrisville: First listed in the July 1919 Journal. The First and Second Readers were Ernest W. And Jessie S. Gates. Mr. and Mrs. Gates joined The Mother church in 1917. Mrs. Gates left the Congregational Church; Mr. Gates had not been a member of a church before becoming a Christian Scientist. He passed away in 1942, the year the Society disbanded; Mrs. Gates passed away in 1956.

Middlebury, 1941

Town and gown mixed in this college town from the beginning; when Professor David K. Smith arrived in 1950, it was usual for the First Reader to be an adult and the Second Reader a student. While still students at Middlebury, for example, Janet Bogart Phinney and Allison (Skip) Phinney were charter members of the Society when it officially formed in 1954. Other charter members who lived in Middlebury were Pauline E. Bibby and Harriette H. Steele.

Mary E. Burpee lived in Addison; Jean W. and Patricia Jaffe in Cornwall; Fanny Ekman in Bristol, Narma C. Leavitt in Weybridge; Lois T. Patterson, Theda H. Stalker, and William A. Stalker in Shoreham. For Gaydell H. Maier we have no address.

Professor Smith recalls that "the early meetings were held in the home of a Mrs. Cushman, whose husband was the Town Clerk of Middlebury. At the time of the 1954 Society status, there were several class taught Scientists and a substantial number of Mother Church members. The group has met at the Community House since before 1950. The Reading Room was begun in 1987."

Jan and Skip Phinney recall finding the Society members extremely interesting and "real" folks. They remember apple growers, a retired teacher with a European background, a Centenarian widow of an American Indian who drove a touring car with window shades, commuting down from Vergennes, and picking up students on the way.

A former teacher at Robert College in Istanbul, Turkey, is remembered for using a sterling silver-tipped cane, and for hostessing young Scientists at her apartment where healings were shared. One of the adult members was married to a local minister whose parents had been killed by the same Indians who had "adopted" him.

Jan Bogart Phinney introduced two lecturers while living in Middlebury. She recalls, "...that both wore tails and spats." One, lecturing for the Middlebury College Organization in a classroom, smelled cigarette smoke from down the hall, and would not continue with his lecture until the smokers stopped (or left the building). Another time, while Jan was in the middle of an introduction, she mentioned the name of the lecturer, who, when he heard his name "shot out of his chair and Jan screamed."

Today, Janet Phinney is a practitioner in Reading, Massachusetts, and Allison W. Phinney, Jr., is a teacher of Christian Science, former manager of the Committees on Publication, and editor of the Journal, Sentinel, and Herald.

Poultney, 1951

Early church records indicate that the first Scientists in the area met in each other's homes. It was not until 1955 that Poultney had its first listing in the Journal, giving the time of the Sunday service as 11, Sunday school at 11, Wednesday evening meeting at 8, and a Reading Room open on Thursday afternoons from 2 to 4. The congregation met in rented rooms in the downtown area until 1960 when their own building was completed. In 1956, the group incorporated under the laws of the state of Vermont having already earned Society status from The Mother Church.

Some of the early members were: Blowdwyn Barlow (Mrs. Charles), Lillian R. Casola, Mr. and Mrs. Gerald Da Costa, Gray Hulett, Ellis Rowlands, Nellie B. Sheeler, and Stella Tyler. It was a gift from the estate of one William Farnham which provided necessary funds for the purchase of a building lot in 1958. Ellis Rowland, a member was also an architect, and the building which is on the site today was designed by him.

Woodstock, 1961

Seventy-five years later (i.e., after the seeds of Christian Science took root in St. Johnsbury), Elizabeth Ferris, a Christian Scientist from Milford, Connecticut, established a second home in the Woodstock area and began holding Sunday services in her living room. She advertised these Sunday services in local papers and put notices on local bulletin boards. Her daughter often made the 300-mile round trip to serve as Second Reader. Very soon, they grew to six "regulars" and had a Sunday school as well.

Even though it was not until 1961 that formal church services were held close to the center of Woodstock, it was as early as 1911 that a Society was recognized by The Mother Church in Barnard, just ten miles north of the Woodstock Village Green. For several years, starting about 1907, Woodstock area Scientists met in homes to read the Sunday service together. Two sisters, Miss Earlie Sacred Chase, C.S., and Miss Lillie Rivers Chase, C.S. were Journal-listed in Barnard in 1907, and were active in the Barnard Society through 1915.

In 1919, a resident of Woodstock had a testimony in the Journal, which is reprinted at the close of this report. And in the 1940s both Mrs. Ruth Shenk Hawkes, CS, and Mrs. Belle M. Vaill, CS, were listed practitioners in Woodstock. There is some reason to believe that they held Sunday church services open to the public while they were active in Woodstock. An official church report states:

> By the fall of 1961, Mrs. Ferris felt the time had come to hold services in a more public place, where a sign could be visible on the sidewalk, and she

rented a room on the second floor [in the downtown area].

During all these months, the services were conducted with the utmost regard for proper form; the order of services given in the <u>Manual</u> was followed to the letter; and every effort was made to have those Sundays and Wednesdays real, honest-to-goodness church services, in spite of the bare little room with the wooden chairs.

By the fall of 1962, the little group had grown to eight regular attendants, with five or six children in the Sunday School. One devoted member who was elected to the post of Second Reader, played the little pump organ for the hymns and sang a solo as well.

They expanded their rented church space in 1964 to begin operating a Reading Room and, in 1965, the following first members were accepted by The Mother Church as a formal Christian Science Society:

    Connie Apte   Besse Deerson
    Elizabeth G. Ferris   Margaret Gage
    George Harvey   Ruth Leonard
    Elizabeth Graves Seaholm Cora White
    Joan Whiteside   Jean Zeller
            Anne Zillessen

They gave their first Christian Science lecture that year.

The next step was the purchase and renovation of their own building, and as in Brattleboro, the first service was held on Thanksgiving Day -- 1971 in Woodstock, 1920 in Brattleboro. When a practitioner moved to the area in 1976 (Jane Willis, C.S.), there were sufficient members, an active Reading Room, and

church services held twice weekly so that they became First Church of Christ, Scientist, Woodstock.

The members made special efforts to be recognized as an active and welcome church home in the community. For example, when the mainline churches decided to hold ecumenical Thanksgiving Day services, they invited the Christian Scientists to participate. At first, they were just asked to read a Bible selection, but the Scientists felt they should contribute to the ecumenical service the same type of "food" used at their own church, hence, they gave correlative readings from the Bible and Science and Health. The Scientists held their own Thanksgiving Day service as well, following the Bible Lesson Sermon in The Christian Science Quarterly.

Also, during the early years of the Society, the Christian Scientists were invited to participate in a special Lenten program -- a series of Friday meetings, which were hosted one by one by the Woodstock churches. The Christian Scientists shared the platform with area ministers, asking one to read and lead the first hymn, and another to read and lead the last hymn. The meeting otherwise was patterned after their testimony meetings with correlative readings on a single topic from the Bible and the Christian Science textbook, and spontaneous remarks about healing through prayer from members of the congregation.

In the June 1919 issue of the Journal, Everett P. Ashley of Woodstock, Vt. had a testimony. Excerpts follow:

> I first heard of Christian Science about thirty years ago, and nineteen years ago, when in California, I met a lady who told me about a

wonderful healing she had experienced as a result of reading "Science and Health with Key to the Scriptures" by Mrs. Eddy. I became interested enough to buy a copy of the book and tried to read it, but could not get much out of it; however, I did not try very hard, as I thought I was well and happy. Soon afterwards I came east and left the book at my brother's home. In the years that followed I had three operations and was finally brought to a place where "man's extremity is God's opportunity." I was led to Christian Science again and this time I was ready for the truth. After my first visit to a practitioner, in the fall of 1914, I commenced to improve, and in six weeks had regained normal weight. My healing in a way was slow, but that made me work all the harder to overcome the discords, such as stomach, bowel, and nasal catarrhal conditions. These faded into their native nothingness as I found that resentment is not a quality of God, good, and that God is Love. About two years ago I was able to give up glasses, which I had used for twenty-three years. Other ailments have been overcome also, including asthma, colds, headaches, and chapped hands.

I am very thankful for membership in The Mother Church and that I have had the experience of class instruction, which is a great help to me in demonstrating this blessed truth for myself and others. For the last four years the Bible and Mrs. Eddy's writings, together with the Christian Science periodicals, have been my daily companions, and I have had great help and protection by reading and studying the Lesson-Sermon each morning before going to my business.

Christian Science

Editor's Note

We discovered that while all the Vermont branches had kept a record of their meeting places, none -- including the Society to which the Editor belongs -- had recorded the healings of the members as part of each Society's or Church's history. We were able to find thirty-seven testimonies by Vermonters which appeared in early volumes of the Journal and Sentinel, but none of the branches' histories included or referenced these healings. Yet Mrs. Eddy stated, as quoted in Volume 114, No. 9, of the Journal: "I retain my conviction that the greatest need that our Cause has is better healers. Those of experience, Christian Character, and ability are more needed, much more to fill this appointment in proof of C.S. than to build up churches."

Taking that statement in the literal sense, we Vermonters are beginning to acknowledge that our histories should focus more on the healing work done by our members than on the work we have done on our church buildings.

SECTION FOUR

FRUITAGE

The First Twenty-three Practitioners:
   1885-1900

The First Three Teachers:
   1904 & 1907

Seventeen Practitioners & Three
   Teachers: 1907

Twelve Practitioners & Two Teachers:
   1926

Eighteen Practitioners & One Teacher:
   1944

 Christian Science

Practitioners & Teachers in Twenty-four Towns

Twenty-seven Testimonies: 1897-1930

Vermont's First Twenty-Three Practitioners 1885-1900

<u>May 1885</u>

Ellen E. Cross, C.S.
Waterford

Ellen Cross was nine years old when her family moved to Waterford, a town just south of St. Johnsbury. In 1883 she had a healing in Christian Science, and the following year took Primary Class instruction from Julia Bartlett, C.S.D., who was her practitioner. In 1885 she took Primary Class from Mrs. Eddy, and in 1886 received Normal Class instruction with Mrs. Eddy. Beginning in April 1887, she was listed as Ellen E. Cross, C.S.D., and had moved to Syracuse, NY, where she practiced and taught until 1893, when she moved to Baltimore, MD. [See the Journal, Vol. 18, page 688.] In 1903, she was called twice to assist Mrs. Eddy at Pleasant View. There is no record of her returning to Vermont after 1887.

July 1885

Mrs. T.H. Hale, C.S.
Montpelier

Mrs. Hale was listed in Boston from February to June 1885 and was subsequently listed in Montpelier from July 1885 through April 1886. We do not know where she went next.

November 1885

Mrs. Mary E. Morse, C.S.
Brattleboro

In the February 1885 Journal, Mrs. Morse is listed in Cambridgeport, Massachusetts. Then, ten months later was listed in Vermont. Her last Vermont listing was in the May 1887 Journal.

July 1889

D. Elmer Goding, C.S.
Mrs. Lottie A. Goding, C.S.
North Pomfret

Two years later, their address was West Rutland; in 1894, they were listed in West Randolph. [Perhaps, W. Rutland was a typographical error.] Mr. Goding attended Edward A. Kimball's Normal Class in 1899 but did not receive a certificate to teach. Apparently in 1893-94, the Godings held the Sunday service and Sunday school in their home in West Randolph. The February 1902 Journal lists them both in Malden,

Massachusetts. There is no record of them returning to Vermont.

January 1892

>Mr. and Mrs. Wm. J. Moore, C.S.
>33 Pearl Street, St. Johnsbury

Their card in the Journal listed them as above for 1892 through 1894. We do not know where they went after they left St. Johnsbury.

November 1893

>Mrs. Elsie A. Flood, C.S.
>McIndoe Falls

Mrs. Flood had Primary Class with M. Anna Osgood, a pupil of Mrs. Eddy's. She was a founding member of the St. Johnsbury Society; McIndoe Falls is a small town on the Connecticut River a few miles south of St. Johnsbury.

>Mrs. Laura W. Burt, C.S.
>8 Pearl Street - St. Johnsbury

Mrs. Burt also had Primary Class with M. Anna Osgood, a pupil of Mrs. Eddy's. She was also a founding member of the St. Johnsbury branch and, like Mrs. Flood, was a long-time member. In the Fall of 1907, Mrs. Burt and her husband, Byron, were asked by Mrs. Eddy to meet with her at Pleasant View. She asked Mr. Burt how he came into Christian Science, and he said it was because of his wife's healing. She also asked him about his love of horses as she needed a new driver.

Christian Science

Satisfied that they would be helpful to her, Mrs. Eddy engaged them to assist with her move on January 26, 1908, from Concord to Chestnut Hill.

Mrs. Burt returned to Vermont to prepare for the move to Chestnut Hill, but Mr. Burt stayed on, living in the stable and caring for the horses. On February 9, when he didn't show up in time to take Mrs. Eddy on her daily drive, he was found dead in bed. Apparently Mr. Burt had a heart problem and had had a heart attack during the night. A member of the household noted that what Mrs. Eddy placed in *The First Church of Christ Scientist and Miscellany* on page 236, line 24, referring all students of Christian Science to a statement about mental malpractice in *Science and Health*, was done as a consequence of Mr. Burt's untimely death.

<u>May 1894</u>

Mrs. Mary Waite Warren, C.S.
West Georgia

About 1886, Mary Waite Warren's mother wrote to Mrs. Eddy requesting a teacher be sent to Vermont. Mrs. Eddy sent Julia Bartlett, and Mrs. Warren (then Miss Waite) took Primary Class instruction from Miss Bartlett. West Georgia is half way between St. Albans and Burlington.

Vermont

November 1894

William Clark, C.S.B.
52 Main Street, Barre

Mr. Clark had Primary Class instruction in 1888 with Mrs. Eddy but did not receive a degree and was ineligible to teach. He was one of the charter members of the Barre branch. He was listed in Barre until 1899, then moved from Vermont. For a brief time he served Mrs. Eddy at Pleasant View as a gardener. It was his healing of Civil-War related injuries that so impressed his friend, the homeopathic physician Ebenezer Foster, that Dr. Foster became a student of Mrs. Eddy's, and in 1888 she made him her adopted son.

January 1896

J.W. Keyes, M.D., C.S.
Mrs. Isabella B. Keyes, C.S.
21 South Main St., Rutland

Dr. and Mrs. Keyes were not listed in Vermont after December 1896 and in December 1902 reappeared in the Journal in Washington, D.C.

The Year 1897

Mrs. Helen B. Ross, C.S.
Rutland

She had telephone #151. See further information under the heading "Vermont's First Three Teachers."

Christian Science

Mrs. Ida M. Green, C.S.
Rochester
Office hours 2-5 except Fridays.
Nearest branch, Randolph.

Miss N. A. Leete, C.S.
Albany

Closest branch, Newport. No listing for Miss Leete in Vermont in 1898, but back in 1900 using full name: Miss Nancy A. Leete, C.S., still in Albany.

The Year 1898

Sylvester C. Hayford, C.S.
7 Cummins St., Montpelier

Listed under the Branch Church section as the First Reader in Barre, and advertisement read that he was in his office Wednesdays in Barre.

Charles's. Van Auker, C.S.
Ripley Block, Rutland

He was listed in Rutland until 1900, and we do not know where he served after he left Vermont. He had a poem -- "Christ's Festal Joys" in the 1919 Journal [Vol. 37, page 447.]

Vermont

The Year 1899

Frank A. Walker, C.S.
Mrs. Rose F. Walker, C.S.
37 Spaulding St., Barre

The Walkers were very active in both Barre and Montpelier for their entire service to the Cause of Christian Science. Mrs. Walker took Normal Class and taught in Vermont from 1907 through 1951. See further information under the heading "Vermont's First Three Teachers."

The Year 1900

Mrs. Nell K. Shipman, C.S.B.
Montpelier

Because Mrs. Shipman's Primary Class teacher (1888) was Mrs. Eddy, she later was given permission to use C.S.D. instead of C.S.B. See information under the heading "Vermont's First Three Teachers."

Mrs. Lucy Gilman, C.S.
Brattleboro

Mrs. Gilman served for many years in the Brattleboro area.

Christian Science

Mrs. Isabel Shackelford, C.S.
Brattleboro

Mrs. Shackelford moved to Pennsylvania in 1902.

Vermont's First Three Teachers

The Year 1904

Mrs. Nell K. Shipman, C.S.D.
Montpelier

Mrs. Shipman, aunt of Emma Shipman, C.S.D., received Primary Class instruction from Mrs. Eddy in 1888, and in 1904 applied for, and received her designation as a C.S.D. We do not know when she taught her first class, but assume it was in 1904 or 1905. There were four Vermonters in Mrs. Eddy's 1888 class. Mrs. Shipman, her sister-in-law Mrs. Dillingham, William Clark, and a Mrs. Ambrose B. Averil. Neither Mrs. Dillingham nor Mrs. Averil were listed practitioners in Vermont.

Vermont

<u>The Year 1907</u>

Mrs. Helen B. Ross, C.S.B.
Rutland

Mrs. Ross had Primary Class with Eugene Greene, C.S.D. in 1904, and Normal Class with him in 1906, and taught her first class in 1907.

Mrs. Rose F. Walker, C.S.B.
Barre

Mrs. Walker received Primary Class instruction twice; from Mary W. Munroe, C.S.D. in 1895, and from Eugene Greene, C.S.D. in 1905. Mr. Greene was her Normal Class teacher in 1906, the same class taken by Mrs. Ross of Rutland. Mrs. Walker taught her first class in 1907. Sometime after her husband passed away she moved to Montpelier. She was listed in the <u>Journal</u> through 1951, and is, to this day, the last teacher in Vermont. Like Mrs. Ross, Mrs. Walker had a telephone; her number was 155-11.

Seventeen Practitioners & Three Teachers in 1907

Barnard [nearest church in Randolph]
    Miss Earlie Sacred Chase, C.S.
    Miss Lillie Rivers Chase, C.S.
Barre
    Mrs. Rose F. Walker, C.S.B.
Burlington
    Mrs. Mary E. Foster, C.S.
    Mrs. May Bennett Jones, C.S.
Essex Junction [nearest church in Burlington]
    Mrs. Charlotte Bowman, C.S.
Montpelier
    Mrs. Nell K. Shipman, C.S.D.
Randolph
    Mrs. Lizzie B. Messer, C.S.
Rutland
    Mrs. Esther T. Abraham, C.S.
    Mrs. Stella Hadden Alexander, C.S.
    Mrs. Helen's. B. Ross, C.S.B.
St. Albans
    Miss Margaret J. Axtell, C.S.
    Mrs. Anna B. Hale, C.S.
    Miss Jane E. Rankin, C.S.
St. Johnsbury
    Mrs. Laura W. Burt, C.S.
    Mrs. Harriet J. Moore, C.S.
    Miss Katherine Puffer, C.S.

Vermont

Twelve Practitioners & Two Teachers in 1926

Barre
    Mrs. Blanche R. Meaker, C.S.
Brattleboro
    Miss Theodosia Boone, C.S.
    Mrs. Lucy Gilman, C.S.
Burlington
    Mrs. Maude Harrod, C.S.
    Miss Early Dawn Hoag, C.S.
Montpelier
    Mrs. Julia Ida Flint, C.S.
    Mrs. Rose F. Walker, C.S.B. [Formerly in Barre]
Rutland
    Mrs. Maude Primm Prowse, C.S.
    Mrs. Helen Ross, C.S.B.
St. Johnsbury
    Mrs. Ida Fuller Moore, C.S.
    Mrs. Jessie A. Stanley, C.S.
Springfield
    Mrs. Susie Holmes Morse, C.S.

Christian Science

Eighteen Practitioners & One Teacher in 1944

Barre
    Mrs. Blanch R. Meaker, C.S.
Bellows Falls
    Mrs. Eunice H. Dizer, C.S. (moved to NJ)
    Mrs. Kathrina D. Haines, C.S.
Bennington
    Mrs. Minnie L. Peckham, C.S.
Brattleboro
    Mrs. Belle Byington Schoenfield, C.S.
Burlington
    Mrs. Dora M. Clark, C.S.
    Mrs. Maude C. Harrod, C.S.
    Mrs. Jeannette Stewart Worden, C.S.
Montpelier
    Mrs. Rose F. Walker, C.S.B.
North Bennington
    Miss Evelyn Paine, C.S.
Norwich
    Mrs. Laura T. Carter, C.S.
Putney
    Mrs. Saidee W. Peckerman, C.S.
Rutland
    Mrs. Irene Cheney, C.S.
    Ross H. Maynard, C.S.
South Strafford
    Mrs. Edna Coates Snow, C.S.
Springfield
    Mrs. Caroline E. Lovell, C.S.
Woodstock
    Mrs. Ruth Shenk Hawkes, C.S.
    Mrs. Belle M. Vaill, C.S.

Practitioners & Teachers in Twenty-four Towns

Between 1885 and 1944, we have located practitioners who advertised in the <u>Christian Science Journal</u> from the following towns scattered throughout all of Vermont.

Albany
Barnard
Barre
Bellows Falls
Bennington
Brattleboro
Burlington
Essex Junction
McIndoe Falls
Montpelier
North Bennington
North Pomfret
Norwich
Putney
Randolph
Rochester
Rutland
South Strafford
St. Albans
St. Johnsbury
Springfield
Waterford
West Georgia
Woodstock

Christian Science

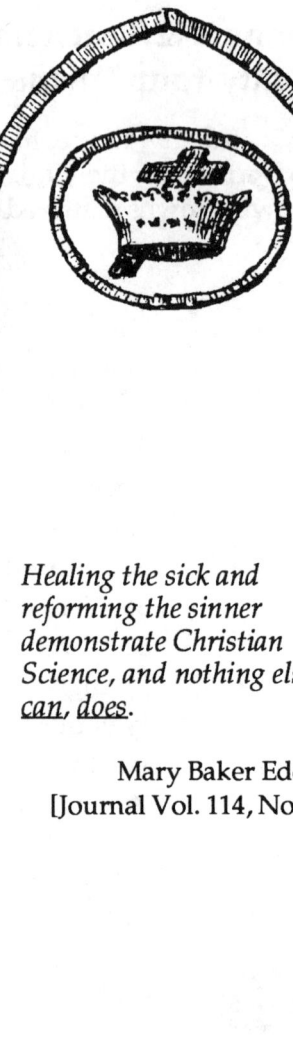

Healing the sick and reforming the sinner demonstrate Christian Science, and nothing else <u>can</u>, <u>does</u>.

Mary Baker Eddy
[Journal Vol. 114, No.9]

Selected Testimonies

    In addition to the ten testimonies that appear throughout Sections One and Three, we have chosen these twenty-seven written by Vermonters that appeared in the <u>Journal</u> and the <u>Sentinel</u> between 1897 and 1930. The first two appear today in "Fruitage" in our textbook. Mrs. Martha E. Porter (who became Mrs. Charles Peck) had her testimony in the <u>Sentinel</u> of August 6, 1904. Mr. Peck's testimony appeared originally in the March 1907 <u>Journal</u>. We have used the original spelling, sentence structure, and treatment of the textbook with (and sometimes without) quotation marks.

RUPTURE AND OTHER SERIOUS ILLS HEALED

When I took up the study of Christian Science nearly three years ago, I was suffering from a very bad rupture of thirty-two years' standing. Sometimes the pain was so severe that it seemed as if I could not endure it. These spells would last four or five hours, and while everything was done for me that could be done, no permanent relief came to me until I commenced reading Science and Health with Key to the Scriptures. After I had once looked into it I wanted to read all the time. I was so absorbed in the study of the 'little book' that I hardly realized when the healing came, but I was healed, not only of the rupture, but also of other troubles, -- inflammatory rheumatism, catarrh, corns, and bunions.

I would never part with the book if I could not get another. I am seventy-seven years old, and am enjoying very good health.

Mrs. M.E.P., St. Johnsbury, Vt.

STOMACH TROUBLE HEALED

I was healed of stomach trouble of many years' standing by reading Science and Health. My condition had reached the stage in which I had periodical attacks that came on with greater frequency. I was a travelling salesman, and it was a common occurrence for me to have to call a physician to my hotel to administer morphine for an acute form of this disease. This became a regular thing at certain places and these attacks always left me worse than before. As a result of the last one I lost a great deal in weight. I had tried many physicians and most of the usual remedies during these years of suffering, without any good result. Finally, as a last resort, I decided to try Christian Science, and I was healed by reading "Science and Health with Key to the Scriptures" by Mrs. Eddy.

My health has been of the best since I was healed, now six years ago. In the family we have depended entirely on Christian Science for our healing, and have ever found it efficacious. We consider the physical healing, however, only incidental to the understanding of God and His goodness. This, together with our increased love for the Bible, is proving most valuable to us. We are humbly trying to live the lives that will prove our gratitude to God, and to our beloved Leader, Mrs. Eddy.

Charles E. Peck, St. Johnsbury, Vt.

Journal May 1897

Like many others, I had been through long years of suffering and was nothing better but grew worse, and like one anciently "had spent all my living and was nothing better but grew worse." No physician gave me any hope of recovery. After ten or twelve years of trial and suffering I was nothing but an object of pity; but through it all I kept hold of the Bible. I read it much, especially the Psalms, the book of Job, and the teaching and healing work of Jesus. I had become convinced that "Jesus Christ, the same yesterday, to-day, and forever" could not change, hence had lost none of his power to bless.

While down sick in bed, as I often was, I received a short letter from friends that read in part like this, "All is Mind, God is your life!" Oh, how changed everything was! God my life! And the spirit of the words of Jacob as he awaked out of his sleep or vision in Bethel, "Surely the Lord is in this place; and I knew it not" (Gen. 28:16), filled my whole being, and the word Immanuel was in my mouth, whether awake or asleep. Before twenty-four hours had passed I was, as another has expressed it, "in a new world." I was asked to tell how I had been helped. I had no story for them, could tell them nothing. I was like the man that was born blind, "One thing I know, that, whereas I was blind, now I see" (John 9:25).

The flight of error with its falsities vanished so quickly I never have been able to trace its flight, only this, God was with me, Immanuel, I was in health! But unlike others I never heard of Christian Science, did not know there was such a book as Science and Health, or a Mary Baker Eddy, but I immediately began to search

for the cause of the great change, and was not long in finding Science and Health, in two volumes. I was exceedingly careful at first, fearing I should be drawn away from the Bible. I was confident that the change had come some way through the Scriptures, because my mind was overflowing with Scripture language. Whether awake or asleep, thought kept the same channel. It was really quite hard for me to realize that I had any need of Science and Health, but by my friend's advice I concluded to purchase the two volumes and very cautiously began to read and compare with the Holy Bible. While reading I began to experience a new light, a reality in the Scriptures, and although ten years have passed I am in health and now am conscious that the Holy Bible and our text-book are inseparable. I am thankful not only for Science and Health, but for all the writings of Mary Baker Eddy.

K.G., Bradford, Vt.

Sentinel October 26, 1899
"To Students" By Emma C. Shipman

While the following was written as an article, it's really a testimony; of course the "girl" in line two is Emma Shipman, herself.

To illustrate the benefit students may derive from Christian Science, I will relate what it did for one student. The one of whom I speak is a girl who had not

been strong from childhood. She was extremely fond of her books and studies, but her school life was frequently interrupted by ill health, which so increased that in the last months of preparation for college she was forced to go from each recitation to her bed; yet when suffering from the great pain or weariness, the thought of her beloved studies would send her back to school.

She began her college work in Boston [at Boston University]. There she met Christian Scientists, attended the Christian Science service, and commenced the study of Science and Health; from this time her life was entirely changed. She grew well and strong. The studies which before had been a burden now became a pastime. Her love for books has increased, so that two, the Bible and Science and Health, have become her constant companions.

In Science and Health she has found a philosophy so broad and high that it meets every human need; a history which is that of the upward march of mind; a science which is exact and unchangeable; a botany which is the analysis and classification of the flowers of thought; a physiology which gives perfect health; a language which is the new tongue spoken of by Jesus in his last commission to the disciples; and a glorious mathematics, even the infinite calculus of divine Love.

By proving the problems in this book, each one may find his true self as the reflection of infinite Intelligence [Upper case "I" in the original.] and Life eternal.

Sentinel February 8, 1900

I was in poor health for eight years and grew worse all the time, until at last I went to a hospital in Montreal and submitted to an operation. This left me in a worse condition in some ways than I was before. That was in November 1894. We lived in Canada at that time, but the next summer we came to Vermont to take care of an old gentleman whose daughter is a Christian Scientist and is away from home all the year, except during the month of August.

I did not know anything about Christian Science. I remember telling my husband that I supposed Miss C. would preach her Spiritualism all the time.

By this time I had ceased to use medicine of any kind, having lost all faith in it, and was convinced that nothing but God could heal me. I could not believe that God was the author of sickness, but I thought I ought to be reconciled to my lot as long as I did not have faith enough to be healed. I prayed all the time for health, and believed I could find it if I only knew how. I felt discouraged and worried all the time.

This was my condition when Miss C. came home in August 1896. I saw right away that she was happy and in good health; but to my surprise she did not mention her "Spiritualism" to me until I became very anxious to know what her belief was. One morning I introduced the subject, and found her willing to talk.

I shall always remember the talk we had that morning. I accepted some ideas very readily, but when she told me about "Science and Health with Key to the Scriptures" I thought I would be on my guard, and not be led astray. However, I decided to read the book and

see if I would be healed. I could not understand it, but I continued to read, for I was determined to give it fair trial. In two days I was very much stirred up. I would lay the book aside, thinking I would let it alone, but in a few minutes would pick it up and read again. The third day I began to get better, but did not say anything about it, for fear I would get worse again. In about a week I became aware that a cloud was lifted from my mind. I felt happier than I had for years, and was free from worry. Then I said I was getting better. I continued to study, for I knew I was being healed. I knew very little of the value of Science and Health. Although I was much better, I was not "every whit whole," and had many battles with error, but Truth was always victor. Last March I began to help others, and have found God a very present help .

How often my heart goes out to our dear Mother! We can never appreciate her as we ought, until we take up the cross ourselves. Then we can realize a little of what she has done for us.

I am now a well, happy woman, and am learning how to love my brother better, for God is the Father of all.

Science and Health is becoming dearer to me every day. I study the Lesson-Sermons, and find them a great help. I take the <u>Journal</u> and <u>Sentinel</u>.

Mrs. Christina A. MacJuer, Waterford, Vt.

Journal July 1900

Among my earliest childhood recollections are those of having the eyes treated and protected from the light by shades.

I think it was in the year 1872 that a noted specialist of Boston was consulted. He said there were ulcers on the eyeballs which, unless cured, would injure the sight.

He prescribed a medicine which seemed to overcome the trouble so that it did not appear for weeks or for a few months at a time, but then the ulcers would return.

This was but one form of the error which, to mortal sense, gave indescribable suffering. Many physicians were sought, among them three specialists -- counted among the best -- noble philanthropists, but they had not the secret of healing; so conditions remained much the same, sometimes confining me to a dark room, limiting educational privileges, and narrowing prospects in all ways.

In August of 1893, tired of semi-invalidism and the fruitless efforts of doctors to heal, I began to ask, What is Christian Science? Is it right? for in thought I had confounded it with mesmerism, spiritualism, or some other ism which I counted as evil, judging from their fruits. When assured that the power was all of God, I felt that it was what had been prayerfully sought but not found in faith or any other so-called healing; and, with but little deliberation, I began taking treatment. Of course all material remedies had to be discarded. They were not many; but a few gods seemed rather precious, among them calomel for the eyes.

Christian Science

Error suggested that I might be blind in consequence, but Truth conquered, and the result is that almost never does the slightest inflammation appear....

Spectacles, which had been depended upon to some extent for more than twenty-five years, and which I was fast coming to feel were needed constantly, were laid aside over a year ago, with something of a struggle, but it is well repaid in returning sight.

Surely words fail to express that debt of gratitude which we owe to our consecrated Leader.

I.M.N., Burlington, Vt.

Journal September 1900

I have thought for some time that it was really selfish of me to continue to read the Christian Science Sentinels and Journals, which I enjoy so much, and not write a word for either of them myself, when I had so much to give thanks for; but as I did not become a Christian Scientist by being wonderfully healed myself, as so many have, I had thought I could not write anything very interesting or wonderful. But then the thought came to me, is it not wonderful, to mortal sense at least, that a family of four should be kept well and happy for fourteen years, without drugs or remedies of any kind excepting the Truth? Of course, physical troubles of various kinds have many times seemed to come to us, but never to stay long, and these were always met by "Divine Love" which we know from our

text-book, "Science and Health with Key to the Scriptures" by Mary Baker G. Eddy, "always has met, and always will meet, every human need."

We have found Christian Science all-powerful, not only in disease and sickness, but in cases of accident, blues, or depression and fear, and is a preventive as well as a cure. It is a religion to **live** by.

I first got interested by the healing of some of the family, and thought then that the healing was all that there was in Christian Science, but I soon learned that that was the least of all the wonderful blessings that it brings to us. I first studied with a student of Mrs. Eddy, and then later with the dear Mother herself, and shall never cease to be thankful to her for showing me the source of all goodness and happiness, and how to live in Truth. I hope always to be faithful to her teachings.

As our family was the only Christian Science family living in the city until now we have one more, my growth has seemed slow, and my practice has not been extensive, but I have always had some patients in my family or among my friends, and have seen cases of croup disappear in less than half an hour, a serious accident to the eye -- while coasting -- quickly healed without leaving a scar or mark of any kind, a case of nervous prostration and a complication of other troubles of two years' or more standing, and treated by many physicians, healed in a few weeks.

All cases have not been as quickly healed as these, but we can never be discouraged when we remember that there is but One Power, and that Omnipotent and Omnipresent.

N[ell].K.S[hipman]., Montpelier, Vt.

Christian Science

<u>Sentinel</u> September 6, 1900

COMPLETELY HEALED BY CHRISTIAN SCIENCE.

I desire to tell of a demonstration related last Sunday morning after the service, by a regular attendant.

The gentleman had suffered since boyhood, whenever he went into the water, from cramps, and he said even from bathing in cold water his flesh would turn purple. The week before the demonstration was related he had worked in the water helping unload and launch a boat that had come on the train to Newport, and was to go on the lake down beyond here to Magog, Canada. He worked three days and a half in the water up to the arm-pits, going home to his dinner without changing his clothes. There has not been the slightest manifestation of cramps, discolored flesh, or cold, and he rejoices to tell what Christian Science has done for him the past year.

About a year ago his wife came for me to tell me he had had a painful shock. The doctor had forbidden him to do any work on account of being liable to bring on another attack of the kind. At the time treatment was asked for every breath he drew caused intense pain. It was about noon when the wife came. I was not able to go to the house then, but told her I would treat him at once and go to see him about four o'clock, which I did. He came out to assist me out of the carriage, and was over at the post office that evening. The law made by the doctor that he should not work was made null and void by the law of Truth. "Science and Health with Key to Scriptures" by Mary Baker G. Eddy, p. 379, says,

"Every law of matter in the body, supposed to govern man, is rendered null and void by the law of God."

Another of our number had a beautiful demonstration last winter in overcoming deafness in the left ear. She kept thinking about it after she went to bed, and all of a sudden the realization came that she could hear. Where, before, if the right ear was buried in the pillow she could not hear a sound, she then heard the clock tick distinctly. The deafness was entirely destroyed at that time.

There are only a few of us in this place, but we have many proofs that the Truth is in our midst.

Elizabeth F. Sleeper, West Derby, Vt.

<u>Sentinel</u> October 4, 1900

Over a year ago I resigned my position in the public schools on account of nervous prostration from overwork. Many weary months were spent in trying to regain my seemingly lost strength, while the errors -- despair and fear -- kept me company. Finally, last winter, divine Love led me to a faithful practitioner, whom I heard talk beautifully and convincingly of sure results in Christian Science, at a Wednesday evening meeting of The Mother Church in Boston. This gentle healer kindly and patiently led me on and out of darkness into the Light. Upon resuming work this spring, I found to my joyful surprise that I was really governing the school by Truth and Love, instead of the

old way, by will-power. I have made many good demonstrations over evil. Especially in the matter of discipline have harmonious and sure results been easily obtained. Many times this term, I have realized Truth for the pupils, in cases of toothache and headache, and in nearly every case, the error has disappeared in a few minutes.

I can work more hours, and need less sleep that the other teachers in the building, and do not feel tired. I am very grateful for help received through the Sentinel and Journal.

D. Macdonald, Readsboro, Vt.

Journal May 1901

In January, 1898, I went to Montreal and submitted to an operation, being under the influence of ether two and one-half hours. I had not been well for a year previous. After the operation, as soon as I was able, I came home, but I could do no work to speak of, only a little light sewing. I was very nervous and kept getting worse for over a year. I was told by a physician in a town adjoining this that I would have to have another operation. I could not bear the thought of it, but did not know of any other way until I was told of Christian Science by a kind friend, and what it had done for her. I began taking treatment June 10, 1899, and July 3, 1899, I came home (I was away when I began treatment), riding fifty-two miles by rail and twelve miles in a carriage.... We live on a farm.... I am very

well indeed, for which I am more thankful than I know how to express. I feel that I do not half appreciate what my healer and others have done for me. I get great help from "Science and Health With Key to the Scriptures." On two occasions I have overcome canker in the mouth. Before I have always resorted to material remedies.

Mrs. Maud Harrington, Eden Mills, Vt.

Sentinel May 15, 1902

"I united with the Baptist Church at the age of fourteen years, and for fourteen years remained an active member in all church work and a teacher in the Sunday School. I am grateful for the dear friends I there found who contributed so largely to my religious education, my love for the Scriptures, and my hungering and thirsting after righteousness. But my heart was not at peace. Thought was tempest-tossed through the warfare of good and evil, flesh and Spirit. The thing that I longed most to know was, "How can I abide in Christ? What is it to abide in Christ?"

Nine years ago (1893), through the healing of a friend, I was led to investigate Christian Science. "Science and Health with Key to the Scriptures" was put into my hand. As I read it I knew I had found what it was to abide in Christ and how to do it....

Now after nine years of toil, struggle, defeat, and triumph I seem again upon the mount and behold again the heaven and earth which God -- Good -- has created.

Peace, that the world never gave and can never take away fills my thought, and Love broods over all. I look back over the way I have come and I see the Red Sea, the desert, and the wilderness; foes within and without.

I can truly say I had need of these experiences. Not once did God forsake me. Though self-will, self-justification, and self-love be as adamant, Love can and does dissolve it. This is the process that has been going on in my consciousness.

Mrs. Rose F. Walker, Barre, Vt.

Sentinel July 10, 1902

I have wished for a long time that I might tell some of the blessings I have received through Christian Science.

Some eight years ago I was healed of diseases which the physicians could not heal. At that time my little boy was healed of an ulcerated artery on his ankle after the doctors had done all they could for him and he was left worse than when they took the case. He is now a well, healthy child.

The spiritual uplifting which I have received is far greater than all else. I am very thankful to God for giving us this beautiful Truth, and to Mrs. Eddy for giving to us Science and Health to teach us how to walk in the light that shines brighter each day.

Mary F. Celley, Calais, Vt.

Journal July 1907

The writer spent some thirty-five years in Vermont before moving to Massachusetts.

On the basis that gratitude seeks expression, I write a few words regarding the way in which God has guided me to a clear view of Truth as revealed in the Bible and "Science and Health with Key to the Scriptures" by Mrs. Eddy. About four years ago my oldest daughter received medical treatment from several physicians, but in vain. By the advice of a friend who had been healed through Christian Science, she applied to a practitioner, and was fully restored in a few days. A year later another daughter was healed. These evidences of God's power and love not only awakened gratitude, but led us all, as a family, to desire and seek more of that life-giving truth by the reading of Christian Science literature; my wife and myself having also had the privilege of class instruction.

During these recent years we have all been kept from any severe sickness, and have been able to meet minor ailments by a realization of God's all-sufficient power. For thirty-five years I have been actively engaged in the Congregational ministry, but as a result of growing convictions regarding the truth and value of Christian Science teaching, I heartily accept those statements of Life, Truth, and Love as embodied and applied in "Science and Health with Key to the Scriptures," and of which the world is to-day in great need.

As an evidence of the increasing open-mindedness shown by other denominations, I quote the reply given by the Lamoille [a northern Vermont county] Association of Congregational

Christian Science

Ministers in answer to my application for withdrawal:-
Jeffersonville, VT. Sept. 26, 1906

Rev. H.M. Perkins.

Dear Brother:--The Association considered your request and instructed the scribe to give you the letter of dismissal. The scribe was also requested to say to you that we have very much enjoyed your fellowship with us in the conference and the Association of Lamoille county, and we regret that your work with us is so soon to close. However, we appreciate your desire to "stand squarely," and to associate and do your work with those Christians with whom you are most nearly in accord and sympathy. The members of Lamoille Association reciprocate your fraternal regard.

Rev. H.M. Perkins, a member of Lamoille Association of Congregational Ministers, in good and regular standing is granted, at his own request, dismissal from this Association with a view of joining the Christian Science Church.

Given by vote of Lamoille Association at Hyde Park, Vt., Sept. 25, 1906.

For the Association,
Henry C. Howard, *Scribe*.

I have thus withdrawn from the former fellowship and become an adherent of the faith which proclaims not only the message, "Go preach the gospel," but also, "Heal the sick."

Rev. Henry M. Perkins, Melrose, Mass.

Journal July 1910

In January, 1908, I contracted a severe cold and had a cough accompanied by very alarming symptoms. After a few days the pain in my lungs became so severe that my husband, who had been having the whole care of me, thought it best to call for help, although we had no fear for the result, knowing that divine Mind governs all. He called a practitioner of our acquaintance, and asked her to go to work immediately on the case. In a few minutes I began to breath easier, fell into a quiet sleep, the first I had had for nearly a week, and in less than an hour woke, all sense of pain was gone and it never returned. The cough and hemorrhage were soon overcome, as were other complications, including extreme weakness, and in a short time I was about my household duties.

We feel very grateful to God, and to our dear Leader, for the wonderful revelation of this great truth that makes free.

Mrs. Angeline H. Towle, St. Johnsbury, Vt.

Journal April 1911

More than five years ago I learned of Christian Science and what it had done for many persons both physically and mentally. I had been out of health much of the time for many years, and had tried different methods of treatment until it seemed there was not one more for me to try. As the illness had returned, and I

was apparently growing weaker daily, I was nearly disconsolate. I then received a letter from a dear friend, who wrote me of the improvement of her health in Christian Science, and I rejoiced, for I felt that there was hope for me once more. After having four weeks' treatment I was able to work and to walk a short distance. At this writing, severe headaches, stomach and heart trouble of a serious nature, and other chronic diseases are but a remembrance of the past. My case is considered a wonderful cure.

I have had good demonstrations of the power of Truth. Christian Science is for me a satisfactory religion: I highly prize "Science and Health with Key to the Scriptures" by Mrs. Eddy, and our other Christian Science publications.

Mrs. Josephine C. Herrick, Montpelier, Vt.

Journal September 1912

A great feeling of gratitude surges over me when I think of my condition now as compared with what it was when I turned to Christian Science for help. Even gratitude seems a poor word to express what I feel, and it is my earnest wish that this testimonial may induce some one who is in need to turn to this source for help, for Truth will not fail.

About three years ago I asked for help in Christian Science for a very bad state of mental depression of long standing. I had tried many other

methods of treatment, various schools of medicine, specialists, etc., and I was in despair, as all had failed. Hundreds of dollars had been spent, I was surrounded by every comfort in my home, husband and children were devoted, I had everything to make life attractive, and yet I was wretched. I felt every morning as though there was not enough in life to be worth living through that day. Words were inadequate to express what I suffered. I dreaded to meet people, as it seemed such an effort to talk, and I could hardly think. Four of my people had gone in this same way, and it seemed inevitable that I should do the same. Life was indeed a burden, and my whole family were under a cloud because of my condition.

But now, thanks to Christian Science, we are in the sunlight of Truth; the clouds have been swept away. I began to improve almost from the first, and was immediately healed of a chronic stomach trouble from which I had not been free for more than ten years. I had been afraid to eat, and confined myself to a very limited diet; but the practitioner told me to eat whatever I wanted, as it would not disturb me, and I found this to be true. I began at once to eat all kinds of food, and have not ever been disturbed for one single day in nearly three years.

I was also healed of many other ills, perhaps the most remarkable healing being that of a stiff shoulder, which was at times painful and always very inconvenient, as I was unable to dress alone or to arrange my own hair. One very noted doctor who examined the shoulder said there was no other way but to have an operation and break the joint, which would be so serious that I would probably not be able to endure it. All these things distressed me more and

more, but after a few weeks' treatment in Christian Science I found, much to my surprise, that I was able to use my arm, and my shoulder soon became perfectly normal. I have had no trouble with it since, which proves to me that the truth reaches the very 'joints and marrow' in its healing work.

I find the study of the Bible, with the text-book, "Science and Health with Key to the Scriptures" by Mary Baker Eddy, very interesting and helpful. My entire family, husband and three children, are all interested, and for nearly three years Christian Science has been our only help in meeting and overcoming all forms of error. I believe we have each got to work out the Science of life, and, as in the case of mathematics, ask for explanations from those who have a better understanding, when we find ourselves unable to do this alone.

Mrs. C.S. Emery, Newport, Vt.

Sentinel June 28, 1913

It is indeed a blessed privilege for Christian Scientists to give expression to their gratitude in our Sentinel and Journal, and I have been helped many times by reading the testimonies coming from grateful hearts. I too have had many proofs of God's love and care for me since this truth came into my life.

A wonderful proof of the protection of Love in these latter days was given me in my experience with a

degenerate who entered my home and held a loaded revolver to my face for ten minutes. My one thought was that of protection for him, and I broke the silence to tell him that as God's child he could not hurt me. Love was indeed close to me that evening, and saved us both. A remarkable healing was manifested in one of my family who had burned her hand according to mortal thought, most seriously. Ten minutes after the practitioner was notified the agonizing pain stopped and no scar remains.

One evening, before the day that I was to sing on an important occasion, I found myself suddenly hoarse, and the sharp pains in my throat became unbearable. I went to bed and tried to treat myself, but even the attempt to swallow caused great suffering. After I had repeated the "Mother's Evening Prayer" by our Leader (Poems, p. 4), I knew that my voice had nothing to do with material manifestations, but was governed by spiritual law. I sang easily and well the next day. I have had many other proofs of the ever efficacy of Christian Science to heal and to save, but for these I have no words; our dear Father-Mother, God knows, however, my intense gratitude for the "Love that guards the nestling's faltering flight," for that light which has revealed the most subtle machinations of mortal mind that have sought to ensnare me.

I owe everything to Christian Science; all my success as singer and teacher is due entirely to the application of the truth found in our text-book, "Science and Health with Key to the Scriptures," given us by our beloved Leader. The peace, joy, and love which has come, and which continues to come to me in my work, is unspeakable. I only pray that I may give out as much as I receive. From a semi-invalid I have grown strong

enough to be the responsibility of keeping together our home, doing work seemingly impossible, and carrying out with success work which, according to human thought, was beyond my ability.

Elsa Owen, Rutland, Vt.

<u>Sentinel</u> November 27, 1915

Since I came into Christian Science many evidences of the ever-presence of divine Love have been vouchsafed me. My father and older brother being ministers, I had early read all the books in a large theological library, and up to a year ago had read the Bible through twenty-three times. During college days, inspired perhaps by my father's favorite quotation, "Prove all things; hold fast that which is good," I became familiar with many of the works of our greatest free-thinkers, and went into slum work and all sorts of work among the poor, hoping to find that larger life for which I was longing but which always seemed just around the corner. At last, weary and discouraged, I dropped into "going it blind," with the hope that in some future life the answer would be revealed. With this submission came a corresponding gradual loss of health, until I was practically a wreck. This state of things continued for several years, and though still young I was doomed by doctors of all schools to worry along in semi-invalidism under several incurable ailments.

Three years ago a good chance to study art came to me, and I went into it so eagerly that all the symptoms of ill health asserted themselves in force, and at last while trying to paint a ceiling I fell from the platform in agony. I was unable to rise from my bed for several days, and then, though believing Christian Science to be of the devil and the great error of this age, to please the people I was with I let them take me to a practitioner. She talked with me for two hours, and though I did not understand much that she said, when I left, to my great astonishment, the pain and weakness were gone. In three treatments I was feeling young and buoyant again, while many so-called incurable ailments, supposedly inherited, had disappeared for good. Most important of all, a great happiness, a constant expectation that the best is yet to be, possessed me. That dear old book, the Bible, so much pondered and so well understood, as I supposed, now opened up with new meaning, and ever since then I have been realizing that "of the increase of his government and peace there shall be no end."

For the Lesson-Sermons, the Christian Science publications, class instruction, and church membership, I cannot be too thankful; and before the example of patient self-abnegation, steadiness of purpose, and wonderful insight of that great woman our beloved Leader, Mrs. Eddy, I bow in speechless admiration. It has been my privilege to realize the truth for myself and others many times, and always with me, even in the hours of desperate struggle, is that needy sense of increase. How glad I am that Christian Science reached me so soon!

Grace M. Bosworth, Bristol, Vt.

<u>Sentinel</u> February 5, 1916

In January, 1911, I first read "Science and Health with Key to the Scriptures" by Mrs. Eddy, at the urgent request of a dear one in California who wrote over and over again of a God who is Love, of the peace "which passeth all understanding," and told me of the "Key" which unlocks the treasures of the Bible so they can be understood clearly. Sorrow, suffering, and despair had weighed me down till I did not want to live. A specialist in Boston said there was no help for me, that I would soon be entirely deaf. Then a certainty that I was fast growing blind came upon me, and terrible headaches added to the blackness; but the worst was the passing on of my little boy. Life was unbearable and I felt I should soon be crazy; but divine Love sent help. I read Science and Health and the headaches ceased forever. The darkness lifted, and all was light; other ills disappeared, the great sorrow was lifted, and Love healed the wounds. Then my hearing was restored. I attended a Christian Science lecture in 1913 and heard every word. I rejoice that I can see and hear; but to me the best of all is the great love and peace which has come, the knowing that God is Love and that He is our Father-Mother.

It was proven for five of us that as God does not send anything but good, we need not have any disease. My son came home with the mumps on both sides of his face, but the swelling went down, and much to every one's surprise none of us caught this ailment.

I am thankful for the faithful work of our beloved Leader, Mrs. Eddy, and also grateful for the help found in our literature; there is so much in every publication

to help and inspire. With divine help I am trying to live as God would have me.

Marion K. Bond, Union Village, Vt.

Journal April 1916

Although words can never express my heart's deep gratitude, it is a duty and a pleasure to give out to the world what Christian Science has done for me. I was not only raised from helplessness to health, but through my healing of physical disease I have found an ever present and all loving God to lean upon daily through all the trials of what is called mortal life. Many times when my burden seemed too great to be borne longer I had prayed God to take me out of it, thinking that if I could die I would be free from my suffering.

About twenty years ago my condition became so serious that a surgical operation was performed for the removal of an abnormal growth, which however, was not found. I was six months recovering from this ordeal sufficiently to be about, though no benefit was received. I continued in this way for ten years, and at the end of this period had submitted to four surgical operations, three of which were abdominal, and from two of which I barely came forth with my life; yet there was no permanent help, although at intervals I was able to go about and attend to daily duties. I was said to be in a very critical condition, but the everlasting arms were all around me. The next two years I was in bed forty-two weeks, the immediate cause being hemorrhages and

sinking spells. During one of these spells my family and the physician present thought I had passed on. Finally materia medica which had included the service of fourteen physicians, pronounced my case hopeless.

Friends then spoke to my husband of Christian Science. [Possibly about 1906.] We had no faith in it that we were conscious of, but my consent to treatment was given, though without any hope of being healed. I was taken from the hospital on a stretcher, placed in a train, and started for Boston, which was one hundred and twenty miles away. I was there put in the care of loving Christian Scientists (although strangers to me then), and the practitioner was called in. I had been on a rigid diet for eight or more years, and for over three there had been no natural action of the lower digestive organs. I also had what physicians pronounced an incurable hernia, caused from surgical operations. In addition, I was said to be mentally unbalanced.

In four days after Christian Science treatment began I was completely healed of the inaction, and in three weeks found myself perfectly healed of all traces of hernia. After six weeks' treatment I could walk three miles in a day and eat anything I liked. Two weeks later, or at the end of eight weeks, when I met my husband at the South Terminal Station in Boston, there had been such marvelous transformation in my appearance that he scarcely knew me. Indeed there are no words that can express the change in me, and only those who had had like experiences and who have been delivered in like manner can know what our gratitude was and ever is.

My joy was so great at the thought of coming home and being and doing like other people, that I failed to hear and obey fully the loving words of the

practitioner, who asked me to attend church to keep close to the study of Christian Science and to God. I was so content that I did not study much or go to church. The following year I was taken very ill with a malady unknown to me or to my husband. He became much alarmed and called a doctor, who cared for me two weeks and then asked to operate for gall-stones. As I refused, my husband consented to my having Christian Science treatment, and through it I was entirely healed.

Since this healing, Christian Science has been found quite sufficient to meet our ever need, and we are today happy and healthy. I am striving to abide "in the secret place of the most High." My gratitude is not alone for my own healing and uplift, but because through my healing my loved ones also have been gathering into the fold.

Marjorie A. Coxson, Brattleboro, Vt.

While the above testimony may seem to any one who has no understanding of Christian Science almost too marvelous to be true, I am happy to be able to verify every statement in it. Indeed, the half has not been told, for there is much more that could be truthfully said in regard to these healings, and others that both Mrs. Coxson and myself have experienced. I am daily finding the power of infinite Mind to be a source of supply for all needs, and am more than grateful that this healing power has found its way into our lives and home, where all is now peace and harmony, in place of what used to be trouble and sorrow and suffering caused by almost constant sickness. God is an ever present help.

E. Frederick Coxson

Sentinel April 29, 1916

In 1904 I became afflicted with catarrh. After having treatment from four of our local physicians without relief, I went to a specialist in another town, who succeeded in relieving the discharge; but I was left quite deaf, and with a constant roaring sound in my ear that at times was almost unbearable. I then consulted a specialist in a town forty-five miles away, making weekly trips for the treatment. Obtaining no relief, I tried other methods of treatment, but all without result. In February, 1906, I went to Minneapolis, where I was treated for seven weeks by one of the best specialists in the West. He tried everything that medical science could suggest and gave up the case as incurable, saying that an operation might stop the noise, but that I would always be deaf. I came home discouraged and gave up consulting doctors.

From August, 1906, till about the same time in 1907, members of my family were ill continually, so that I became very nervous and my general health much impaired. This condition aggravated the deafness and noises in the head, until it seemed as if I would rather die than live. The first of October, 1907, I went to Boston, stopping in the house of a gentleman who had become a Christian Scientist through his own remarkable healing. At that time I had heard of some of the healings Christian Science had accomplished, though I knew nothing of its teachings and gave the subject little thought or credence. One day, however, I told this gentleman that if he or Christian Science could do anything for my head, I wished he would do it. He said he would gladly try to help me, although he advised me to go to a regular practitioner, as he was only a beginner; but I preferred his treatment. I retired

that night feeling rather disappointed that he did not keep me up and pray over me, or do something, I hardly knew what; but I slept peacefully all night and awoke the following morning well. The noises have never returned and my hearing is normal. I feel that I am completely cured of the trouble.

In August, 1912, I was in Minneapolis again, and at the request of my brother called on the specialist who had treated me, requesting an examination. He pronounced the ear normal. He also said that he remembered my case perfectly, and asked who cured me. When I told him, he only remarked, "I have known of the Christian Scientists doing some very remarkable things." Since this healing I have used no material remedies and have tried to order my life by the teaching of Christian Science.

C.L.M. Bugbee, Newport, Vt.

<u>Sentinel</u> May 13, 1916

The following appeared originally at the close of the testimony. "The above testimony was subscribed and sworn to before a notary public." Signed "Editor."

Just four years ago I was healed in Christian Science of the morphine habit, after having used the drug for eleven years, and being a slave to it for nine years. The drug was first given to me by physicians in

the East for severe attacks of asthma, after every other known remedy had been tried. My parents spent large sums trying to find a cure for this ailment, but nothing relieved the terrible agony until the drug was used. At first there seemed to be no danger that the habit would be formed, as these attacks were many weeks apart; but they soon became more frequent, so that the last eight weeks spent in my eastern home I sat in a chair day and night, the opiate being administered daily. When I left Vermont the physicians gave my husband authority to administer the drug, as he had had much experience in that line. They also expressed much sympathy for me, saying I would always have to take it.

When we arrived in Chicago I was much better, and this was the time to have stopped taking the drug; but my husband being ill the physician told the nurses that they should not take the drug away from me, as it would help to keep me up. It was only a short time before the asthma returned with great severity. Many sad things happened as a result of using this drug, one of which I will mention. My husband and myself were both members of a church in Chicago, and the rector made us many visits. One afternoon when he called he found me suffering from a severe attack of asthma and using the opiate. He said: "I have come to excommunicate you and your husband from the church because you have the morphine habit and your husband is administering the drug; but I will put you on three months' probation, and if at the end of that time you can prove to me that you have given up the drug habit, I will welcome you back to the church." I do not mention this with any feeling of resentment, for the man did what he considered was his duty.

A few months later we arrived in Los Angeles, where my husband passed away in a short time. I was left alone among strangers, in ill health, a so-called "drug fiend," and obliged to earn my own living. Believing that my strength depended upon the drug, I used no discretion, and this of course prevented my holding a position for any length of time. This continued for five years, until I was cured in Christian Science. My healing was beautiful and complete. When I went to see the practitioner, I was using an enormous amount of the drug, but in less than two weeks I handed all I had of it and everything that went with it over to the practitioner, never expecting to use it again; and I never have. My sense of suffering during the twelve days that followed was very great, and I ate comparatively nothing. I could not sleep and lost greatly in flesh, but I was clear mentally and was not troubled for an instant.

This healing took place in the city of San Diego, Cal., and I shall be very glad to answer any questions regarding it. I have had many tests to prove whether I was really cured, but have stood all these without wavering. Nearly three years ago I married again and came to my present home. My husband has become interested in Christian Science and depends upon it wholly for help. My thankfulness to God and my gratitude to Mrs. Eddy are boundless. If Christian Science were doing no other work in the world today than curing people of the drug habit alone, it truly would be of untold value to mankind.

Mrs. D.H. Switzer, Bellows Falls, Vt.

Journal June 1917

It is with unspeakable thankfulness to God, the giver of all good, and with gratitude to our dearly beloved Leader, Mrs. Eddy, for her spiritual interpretation of the teachings of the Master, that I acknowledge my healing of curvature of the spine. After relying on material remedies for several years and finding no help, I turned to Christian Science and was healed. When I think of what Christian Science has saved me from, of the peace and harmony it has brought into my life, of its gentle ministry in helping me to conquer impatience, hate, and a false sense of personality, I find myself in awe of the power of divine Love, and wish that all the world might share its blessings.

It is wonderful to know that through the power of Truth we can overcome physical and mental discord, but this is as nothing compared with the spiritual healing. The Bible has become a new book to me and money could not buy the understanding of the truth that I have gained through reading the Bible with Science and Health. I am thankful, too that early in life I have been guided into that straight and narrow but well defined path which leads to eternal life, and which grows ever brighter and clearer as I realize that it is the same path which our Master, Christ Jesus, took, and which our Leader has opened anew for all mankind. I have gained not only health and happiness through Christian Science but also a spiritual understanding of this wonderful truth.

May Lynch, Richford, Vt.

Journal September 1919

I have been interested in Christian Science for fourteen years and would like to express my gratitude for the many blessings it has brought into my life. The overcoming of nervous prostration in its worst form, and the healing of a badly sprained ankle, an infected finger, a severe burn on the foot, and a serious attack of influenza, are some of the benefits received. The sense of being always tired has also left me. What means much more to me, however, is the spiritualization of thought, and the better understanding of God and the Bible.

I am trying each day to obey the Master's command, "Let your light so shine before men, that they may see your good works, and glorify your Father which is in heaven." I am truly thankful to God, and grateful to Mrs. Eddy for the unfolding of truth to mankind in this age.

Mrs. Charles C. Nichols, Vergennes, Vt.

Journal June 1919

I wish to add my testimony to the great number being given in the Journal. Eighteen years ago I was healed, by absent treatment in Christian Science, of what my physician called nervous breakdown with the so-called serious ailments. Our youngest child was instantaneously healed of spasmodic croup, just after my own healing, through my understanding of the

truth. Since that time Christian Science has never failed us when it has been properly applied. Sometimes my husband felt the doctor should be called, as he could not understand how anything was being done for the children unless he could see the doctor's potion in evidence. He feels very differently now and is beginning to look into Christian Science a little for himself.

There have been so many healings it is not possible for me to write about them all, but the physical freedom is to me the least of all the blessings, for the peace "which passeth all understanding" is more to be desired than "great riches," and that is here and now revealed in our textbook "Science and Health with Key to the Scriptures," by Mrs. Eddy. Studied in connection with the Bible, which we now love and understand, it will lead us out of the wilderness of materiality into the spiritual understanding of harmony, Life, Truth and Love. We can never be grateful enough to our revered Leader, Mrs. Eddy for making the way so plain for us.

Mrs. Annette M. Martin, Elmore, Vt.

Sentinel December 6, 1930

Many times I have been helped and encouraged by reading the testimonies in our periodicals; and I am glad to express my gratitude for these loving channels, made possible by the wisdom of our beloved Leader, Mary Baker Eddy, for the sharing of our blessings with one another.

Once a wart appeared on the left side of my nose. Never having seen anything like it before, I was filled with fear and asked help of a kind practitioner. The healing was slow, but perfect, not even a trace of the difficulty remaining. Christian Science is for anyone; and the more we use it the better we understand it, and the happier our lives become.

Mrs. Elsa Constans Holden, Burlington, Vt.